Better Homes and Gardens®

pasta

familydinners

Better Homes and Gardens®

pasta

familydinners

JG
PRESS

Copyright © 2011 by Meredith Corporation, Des Moines, IA. All rights reserved.

Published by World Publications Group, Inc., 140 Laurel Street, East Bridgewater, MA 02333, www.wrldpub.com

Library of Congress Cataloging-in-Publication Data

Better homes and gardens pasta family dinners.
    p. cm.
Includes index.
ISBN 978-1-57215-694-4 (cloth); 978-1-57215-740-8 (cloth) -- ISBN 978-1-57215-695-1 (pbk.)
1. Cooking (Pasta) 2. Cookbooks. I. Better homes and gardens. II. Title: Pasta family dinners.
TX809.M17B473 2011
641.8'22--dc22

2010042338

Printed in China
10 9 8 7 6 5 4 3 2 1

Better Homes and Gardens®

Test Kitchen™

Our seal assures you that every recipe in *Pasta Family Dinners* has been tested in the Better Homes and Gardens Test Kitchen®. This means that each recipe is practical and reliable and meets our high standards of taste appeal. We guarantee your satisfaction with this book for as long as you own it.

contents

soups WITH PASTA

Asian Chicken Noodle Soup, *recipe page 12*

mexican chicken MINESTRONE

You can't beat a tasty, slightly spicy soup that cooks up in half an hour!

Prep: 20 minutes
Start to Finish: 30 minutes
Makes: 6 servings

12 ounces skinless, boneless chicken breast halves, cut into bite-size pieces

1 teaspoon chili powder

2 cloves garlic, minced

1 tablespoon vegetable oil

2 (14-ounce) cans low-sodium chicken broth

1 (15-ounce) can black beans, rinsed

1 cup frozen corn

1 cup dried pipette or elbow macaroni

1 (14-ounce) can Mexican-style stewed tomatoes, cut up

Cilantro sprigs

1 In a bowl toss chicken with chili powder. In a 4-quart pot or Dutch oven, cook garlic in hot oil over medium heat for 15 seconds and add chicken. Cook, stirring, 3 minutes.

2 Add broth, 1 cup water, beans, and corn. Bring to a boil, stirring frequently. Stir in pasta. Reduce heat and simmer, covered, 10 minutes or until pasta is tender, stirring occasionally.

3 Stir in tomatoes; heat through. Top each serving with cilantro.

Nutrition Facts per serving: 260 cal., 3.5 g total fat (0.5 g sat. fat), 33 mg chol., 727 mg sodium, 34 g carbo., 22 g pro.

confetti chicken SOUP

Find coconut milk in most large supermarkets. Don't confuse it, however, with (sweetened) cream of coconut, which is used to make mixed drinks.

Prep: 30 minutes
Cook: 6 minutes
Makes: 6 servings

2 **tablespoons cooking oil**

1 **pound skinless, boneless chicken breast halves, cut into 1-inch pieces**

4 **teaspoons grated fresh ginger**

1 **tablespoon red curry paste or ¼ teaspoon cayenne pepper**

1 **teaspoon ground cumin**

8 **cloves garlic, minced**

4 **cups water**

1 **14-ounce can unsweetened coconut milk**

2 **cups shredded carrots**

2 **cups small broccoli florets**

1 **medium red sweet pepper, cut into bite-size strips**

2 **3-ounce packages chicken-flavor ramen noodles, coarsely broken**

2 **cups fresh snow pea pods, tips removed and halved crosswise**

2 **tablespoons soy sauce**

4 **teaspoons lime juice**

1 **cup slivered fresh basil**

⅓ **cup snipped fresh cilantro**

1 In a 4-quart Dutch oven heat 1 tablespoon of the oil. Add chicken; cook and stir over medium-high heat for 3 to 4 minutes or until no longer pink. Remove chicken; set aside.

2 Add remaining oil to Dutch oven. Add ginger, curry paste, cumin, and garlic; cook and stir for 30 seconds. Stir in water, coconut milk, carrots, broccoli, sweet pepper, and noodles (set seasoning packets aside). Bring to boiling; reduce heat. Simmer, covered, for 3 minutes. Stir in cooked chicken, seasoning packets, pea pods, soy sauce, and lime juice; heat through. Stir in basil and cilantro.

Nutrition Facts per serving: 454 cal., 25 g total fat (12 g sat. fat), 44 mg chol., 1,087 mg sodium, 33 g carbo., 26 g pro.

asian chicken NOODLE SOUP

Soy sauce, ginger, and pea pods add an Asian flair to this version of a classic favorite.

Start to Finish: 20 minutes
Makes: 3 servings

- 2 **14-ounce cans chicken broth (3½ cups)**
- 1 **cup water**
- ¾ **cup dried fine egg noodles**
- 1 **tablespoon soy sauce**
- 1 **teaspoon grated fresh ginger**
- ⅛ **teaspoon crushed red pepper**
- 1 **medium red sweet pepper, cut into ¾-inch pieces**
- 1 **medium carrot, chopped**
- ⅓ **cup thinly sliced green onions**
- 1 **cup chopped cooked chicken or turkey**
- 1 **cup fresh pea pods, halved crosswise, or ½ of a 6-ounce package frozen pea pods, thawed and halved crosswise**

1 In a large saucepan combine chicken broth, water, noodles, soy sauce, ginger, and crushed red pepper. Bring to boiling. Stir in the sweet pepper, carrot, and green onions. Return to boiling; reduce heat. Simmer, covered, for 4 to 6 minutes or until vegetables are crisp-tender and noodles are tender.

2 Stir in chicken and pea pods. Simmer, uncovered, for 1 to 2 minutes more or until pea pods are crisp-tender.

Nutrition Facts per serving: 224 cal., 6 g total fat (2 g sat. fat), 58 mg chol., 1,280 mg sodium, 17 g carbo., 2 g fiber, 24 g pro.

pasta and bean CHICKEN SOUP

Canned white beans, canned tomatoes, cooked chicken, and purchased pesto moves soup-making into the express lane. Try this trattoria tip: Place a slice of grilled bread in each bowl and then ladle the soup on top.

Start to Finish: 25 minutes
Makes: 5 servings

3½ cups reduced-sodium chicken broth

1 cup water

1 19-ounce can white kidney beans or Great Northern beans, rinsed and drained

2 cups chopped cooked chicken

1 14½-ounce can diced tomatoes with onion and garlic or diced tomatoes with basil, oregano, and garlic, undrained

1½ cups thinly sliced carrots

1 cup dried ditalini or tiny bow ties (4 ounces)

¼ cup purchased pesto

1 In a large saucepan combine broth, water, beans, chicken, undrained tomatoes, carrots, and pasta.

2 Bring to boiling; reduce heat. Simmer, covered, about 10 minutes or until pasta is tender but firm. Stir in pesto.

Nutrition Facts per serving: 323 cal., 12 g total fat (1 g sat. fat), 46 mg chol., 914 mg sodium, 33 g carbo., 25 g pro.

turkey vegetable SOUP

Pistou—a blend of basil, garlic, Parmesan cheese, and olive oil—is the French counterpart of Italian pesto. Fix extra and use it as you would pesto.

Prep: 30 minutes
Cook: 40 minutes
Makes: 10 servings

1 tablespoon olive oil

1 large onion, chopped

6 cloves garlic, minced

3 14-ounce cans chicken broth

2 cups water

3 medium tomatoes, chopped

1 19-ounce can cannellini beans (white kidney beans), rinsed and drained

1 medium fennel bulb, trimmed and chopped

1½ teaspoons dried thyme, crushed

1 teaspoon salt

½ teaspoon ground black pepper

2 bay leaves

2 cups chopped cooked turkey or chicken

2 medium zucchini, chopped

1 10-ounce package frozen green beans

½ cup dried orzo pasta or other small pasta

Pistou*

Shredded Parmigiano-Reggiano cheese (optional)

1 In a 4-quart Dutch oven heat oil over medium heat. Add onion and garlic; cook and stir until tender. Stir in chicken broth, water, tomatoes, cannellini beans, fennel, thyme, salt, pepper, and bay leaves. Bring to boiling; reduce heat. Cover and simmer for 30 minutes.

2 Stir in turkey, zucchini, green beans, and orzo pasta. Cover and simmer for 10 minutes more or until pasta is tender. Remove bay leaves.

3 Meanwhile, prepare Pistou. Ladle the soup into bowls. Top with Pistou and, if desired, Parmigiano-Reggiano cheese.

***Pistou:** In a food processor or blender, combine 2 cups firmly packed fresh basil leaves (about 2½ ounces), 2 tablespoons grated Parmigiano-Reggiano cheese, 2 tablespoons olive oil, and 6 cloves garlic, halved. Cover and process or blend until finely chopped. Add enough additional olive oil (1 to 2 tablespoons) to thin mixture to desired consistency.

Nutrition Facts per serving: 215 cal., 8 g total fat (1 g sat. fat), 23 mg chol., 848 mg sodium, 24 g carbo., 15 g pro.

Make Ahead: Prepare Pistou as directed. Transfer to an airtight container and chill for up to 24 hours.

turkey ravioli SOUP

Start to Finish: 25 minutes
Makes: 6 servings

6   cups reduced-sodium chicken
    broth

¾   cup chopped red sweet
    pepper (1 medium)

½   cup chopped onion
    (1 medium)

1½ teaspoons dried Italian
    seasoning, crushed

1½ cups chopped cooked turkey
    (8 ounces)

1   9-ounce package refrigerated
    light cheese ravioli

2   cups shredded fresh spinach

    Finely shredded Parmesan
    cheese (optional)

1 In a Dutch oven combine chicken broth, sweet pepper, onion, and Italian seasoning. Bring to boiling; reduce heat. Simmer, covered, for 5 minutes.

2 Add turkey and ravioli to broth mixture. Return to boiling; reduce heat. Simmer, uncovered, about 6 minutes or just until ravioli is tender. Stir in spinach. If desired, sprinkle individual servings with Parmesan cheese.

Nutrition Facts per serving: 246 cal., 7 g total fat (3 g sat. fat), 48 mg chol., 879 mg sodium, 24 g carbo., 22 g pro.

beef goulash SOUP

A single teaspoon of unsweetened cocoa powder contributes a hint of New World uniqueness to an Old World Hungarian goulash. Don't be surprised if your family asks for this soup time and time again.

Prep: 25 minutes
Cook: 30 minutes
Makes: 4 (1½-cup) servings

6 ounces boneless beef sirloin steak

1 teaspoon olive oil

1 medium onion, cut into thin wedges

2 cups water

1 14-ounce can beef broth

1 14½-ounce can low-sodium tomatoes, undrained and cut up

½ cup thinly sliced carrot

1 teaspoon unsweetened cocoa powder

1 clove garlic, minced

1 cup thinly sliced cabbage

1 ounce dried wide noodles (about ¾ cup)

2 teaspoons paprika

¼ cup fat-free dairy sour cream

1 Trim fat from beef. Cut beef into ½-inch cubes. In a large saucepan heat olive oil over medium-high heat. Cook and stir beef in hot oil over medium-high heat about 6 minutes or until beef is browned. Add onion wedges; cook and stir about 3 minutes or until tender.

2 Stir in the water, beef broth, undrained tomatoes, carrot, cocoa powder, and garlic. Bring to boiling; reduce heat. Simmer about 15 minutes or until beef is tender. Stir in cabbage, noodles, and paprika. Simmer for 5 to 7 minutes more or until noodles are tender but firm. Remove from heat; stir in sour cream until combined.

Nutrition Facts per serving: 178 cal., 6 g total fat (2 g sat. fat), 34 mg chol., 400 mg sodium, 17 g carbo., 15 g pro.

beef and ravioli SOUP

This hearty combination of beef, fresh vegetables, and ravioli is perfect for a chilly spring evening.

Prep: 30 minutes
Cook: 30 minutes
Makes: 6 main-dish or
8 side-dish servings

½ **pound boneless top sirloin, cut into ¼-inch dice**

2 **tablespoons flour**

2 **tablespoons butter or margarine, melted**

1 **celery rib, chopped**

1 **carrot, chopped**

1 **onion, chopped**

1 **tablespoon garlic, chopped**

½ **teaspoon thyme**

½ **teaspoon white pepper**

2 **cans (14 ounces each) beef broth**

1 **can (28 ounces) whole tomatoes in juice, chopped**

1 **cup water**

½ **teaspoon salt**

1 **package (9 ounces) refrigerated beef ravioli (or one 8-ounce packaged frozen beef tortellini)**

2 **tablespoons flour**

1 **tablespoon cornstarch**

2 **tablespoons water**

1 Toss boneless sirloin and 2 tablespoons flour in bowl. Melt butter or margarine in large Dutch oven over medium-high heat. Cook until beef is browned; transfer with slotted spoon to bowl.

2 Add chopped celery, carrot, onion, garlic, thyme, and white pepper to Dutch oven. Cook, stirring, 3 minutes, until vegetables are lightly browned. Add beef broth, tomatoes in juice, 1 cup water, reserved beef, and salt. Bring to boil; reduce heat to medium and cook 20 minutes, until vegetables are tender. Add beef ravioli; cook 10 minutes, stirring occasionally.

3 Meanwhile, combine 2 tablespoons flour and cornstarch with 2 tablespoons water in cup until smooth. Stir into soup; bring to boil and boil 1 minute.

Nutrition Facts per serving: 245 cal., 12 g total fat (3.5 g sat. fat), 52 mg chol., 970 mg sodium, 22 g carbo., 13 g pro.

souper SPAGHETTI

No need to boil water; cook the pasta right in the well-seasoned sauce.

Prep: 20 minutes
Cook: 25 minutes
Makes: 6 servings

1 pound lean ground beef

1 medium onion, chopped

1 small green sweet pepper, chopped

1 stalk celery, chopped

1 medium carrot, chopped

1 teaspoon minced garlic

2 14.5-ounce cans diced tomatoes, undrained

2½ cups water

1 13- to 15-ounce jar spaghetti sauce

1 tablespoon sugar

½ teaspoon dried Italian seasoning, crushed

½ teaspoon salt

¼ teaspoon ground black pepper

Dash crushed red pepper

2 ounces spaghetti, broken into 2-inch pieces

Fresh herb sprigs (optional)

1 In a large saucepan or Dutch oven cook meat, onion, sweet pepper, celery, carrot, and garlic over medium heat until vegetables are tender and meat is no longer pink, stirring frequently. Drain excess fat.

2 Add undrained tomatoes, the water, spaghetti sauce, sugar, Italian seasoning, salt, black pepper, and red pepper. Bring mixture to boiling. Add broken spaghetti. Return to boiling. Reduce heat and boil gently, uncovered, for 12 to 15 minutes or until spaghetti is tender. Serve immediately. If desired, top each serving with a fresh herb sprig.

Nutrition Facts per serving: 263 cal., 9 g total fat (3 g sat. fat), 48 mg chol., 960 mg sodium, 28 g carbo., 17 g pro.

italian meatball SOUP

What to do with the leftover packaged meatballs? Another night, pair them with prepared pasta sauce for a quick and classic spaghetti and meatball dinner.

Prep: 15 minutes
Cook: 10 minutes
Makes: 4 servings

1   **14.5-ounce can diced tomatoes with onion and garlic, undrained**

1   **14-ounce can beef broth**

1½   **cups water**

½   **teaspoon dried Italian seasoning, crushed**

½   **of a 16-ounce package frozen Italian-style cooked meatballs**

½   **cup small dried pasta (such as elbow macaroni, orzo, rosamarina, tripolini, ditalini, or stellini)**

1   **cup frozen mixed vegetables**

Finely shredded Parmesan cheese

1 In a large saucepan combine undrained tomatoes, broth, the water, and Italian seasoning; bring to boiling.

2 Add frozen meatballs, uncooked pasta, and frozen vegetables. Return to boiling; reduce heat. Cover and simmer about 10 minutes or until pasta and vegetables are tender. Top each serving with cheese.

Nutrition Facts per serving: 337 cal., 16 g total fat (7 g sat. fat), 42 mg chol., 1,419 mg sodium, 31 g carbo., 18 g pro.

pork and orzo SOUP WITH SPINACH

Boneless pork chops are a great choice for soups. The addition of pasta, fresh herbs, and spinach give a Mediterranean flavor to this meaty soup.

Start to Finish: 50 minutes
Makes: 6 (10½-cups) servings

1½ **pounds boneless pork loin chops, cut into 1-inch cubes**

2 **tablespoons cooking oil**

4 **cups water**

2 **14-ounce cans chicken broth or vegetable broth**

2 **bay leaves**

1 **tablespoon snipped fresh oregano or 1 teaspoon dried oregano, crushed**

1½ **teaspoons snipped fresh marjoram or ½ teaspoon dried marjoram, crushed**

½ **teaspoon salt**

¼ **teaspoon black pepper**

1 **cup bite-size carrot strips (2 medium)**

1 **cup sliced celery (2 stalks)**

¾ **cup dried orzo pasta (rosamarina)**

3 **cups torn spinach or ½ of a 10-ounce package frozen chopped spinach, thawed and well drained**

1 In a 4-quart Dutch oven or kettle cook the meat, half at a time, in hot oil over medium-high heat until brown. Drain fat.

2 Stir in water, broth, bay leaves, oregano, marjoram, salt, and pepper. Bring to boiling. Stir in carrots, celery, and pasta. Return to boiling; reduce heat. Simmer, covered, about 15 minutes or until vegetables and pasta are tender. Discard bay leaves.

3 Stir in spinach. Cook for 1 to 2 minutes more or just until spinach wilts.

Nutrition Facts per serving: 261 cal., 9 g total fat (3 g sat. fat), 62 mg chol., 709 mg sodium, 13 g carbo., 30 g pro.

pasta fagioli WITH SAUSAGE

Prep: 10 minutes
Cook: 18 minutes
Makes: 8 servings

- 2 **tablespoons olive oil**
- ½ **pound sweet Italian sausage, casings removed and discarded**
- 3 **cloves garlic, thinly sliced**
- 3 **large chicken bouillon cubes, dissolved in 6 cups hot water**
- 1 **can (28 ounces) crushed tomatoes**
- 1 **teaspoon dried Italian herb seasoning**
- ¼ **teaspoon onion salt**
- ¼ **teaspoon black pepper**
- 1 **pound ditalini pasta**
- 2 **cans (19 ounces each) cannellini beans, drained and rinsed**
- ½ **cup grated Parmesan cheese**

1 In large saucepan heat oil over medium-high heat. Crumble sausage into saucepan; cook, stirring occasionally, until no longer pink, about 5 minutes. Add garlic; cook 1 minute.

2 Add dissolved bouillon cubes, tomatoes, Italian seasoning, onion salt, and pepper. Bring to boiling over high heat. Stir in pasta. Reduce heat; simmer, stirring occasionally, until pasta is tender, 10 to 11 minutes.

3 Stir in beans; cook until beans are heated through, about 1 minute. Serve immediately with cheese.

Nutrition Facts per serving: 439 cal., 14 g total fat (4 g sat. fat), 22 mg chol., 1,239 mg sodium, 60 g carbo., 16 g pro.

ham, pasta, and bean SOUP

For the broth, use canned chicken broth or dissolve 2 teaspoons instant chicken bouillon granules in 2 cups of boiling water.

Prep: 20 minutes
Cook: 10 minutes
Makes: 4 main-dish servings

1 **15-ounce can navy beans, rinsed and drained**

2½ **cups water**

2 **cups chicken broth**

½ **teaspoon dried marjoram or basil, crushed**

¼ **teaspoon pepper**

1 **cup dried tricolor wagon wheel macaroni or elbow macaroni**

1 **cup cubed fully cooked ham or fully cooked smoked turkey**

1 **medium onion, chopped (½ cup)**

1 **stalk celery, sliced (½ cup)**

1 Using a potato masher, mash about half of the navy beans. Set whole and mashed navy beans aside.

2 In a large saucepan combine water, chicken broth, marjoram, and pepper. Bring to boiling. Add the mashed and whole navy beans, pasta, ham, onion, and celery to the broth mixture. Return to boiling; reduce heat. Simmer, uncovered, for 10 to 15 minutes or until pasta is tender but slightly firm, stirring occasionally.

Nutrition Facts per serving: 275 cal., 3 g total fat (1 g sat. fat), 11 mg chol., 1,090 mg sodium, 40 g carbo., 21 g pro.

macaroni and cheese
CHOWDER

Start to Finish: 30 minutes
Makes: 4 to 6 servings

1 **14-ounce can reduced-sodium chicken broth**

1 **cup water**

1 **cup dried elbow macaroni**

1 **cup frozen whole kernel corn**

1 **cup chopped sliced cooked ham (5 ounces)**

6 **ounces American cheese, cubed**

1 **cup milk**

Shredded cheddar cheese (optional)

1 In a large saucepan bring chicken broth and water to boiling. Add macaroni; reduce heat. Simmer, covered, about 12 minutes or until macaroni is tender, stirring occasionally.

2 Stir in corn, ham, American cheese, and milk. Cook and stir over medium heat until cheese melts. Ladle into bowls. If desired, top individual servings with cheddar cheese.

Nutrition Facts per serving: 393 cal., 18 g total fat (10 g sat. fat), 64 mg chol., 1,338 mg sodium, 35 g carbo., 23 g pro.

basic MINESTRONE

Start to Finish: 30 minutes
Makes: 6 (1⅔-cup) servings

2 cloves garlic, minced

1 medium onion, chopped

1 tablespoon extra virgin
   olive oil

1 large yellow sweet pepper,
   coarsely chopped

1 medium zucchini, coarsely
   chopped

2 14-ounce cans beef broth

2 cups water

1 15-ounce can cannellini
   beans, rinsed and drained

8 ounces fresh green beans,
   trimmed and cut into
   1½-inch pieces (1½ cups)

1 cup dried mostaccioli pasta
   (4 ounces)

¼ cup coarsely chopped fresh
   basil or 2 teaspoons dried
   basil, crushed

2 medium tomatoes, coarsely
   chopped or 1½ cups cherry
   tomatoes, halved

2 cups packaged fresh baby
   spinach leaves

   Shaved Parmesan cheese
   (optional)

① In a 5- to 6-quart Dutch oven cook garlic and onion in hot oil until tender, stirring occasionally. Add sweet pepper, zucchini, beef broth, and water. Bring to boiling. Add beans, pasta, and dried basil (if using); return to boiling. Reduce heat and simmer, covered, for 10 to 12 minutes or until pasta is tender, stirring occasionally.

② Stir in tomatoes, spinach, and fresh basil (if using). Remove from heat. Season to taste with salt and ground black pepper.

③ Top with Parmesan cheese, if desired.

Nutrition Facts per serving: 186 cal., 3 g total fat (0 g sat. fat), 0 mg chol., 621 mg sodium, 34 g carbo., 10 g pro.

creamy carrot AND PASTA SOUP

Fresh ginger and a dash of jerk seasoning—a unique island blend of spices, herbs, and fiery chiles—give this special soup a tropical flair.

Start to Finish: 30 minutes
Makes: 4 servings

- 2 **14-ounce cans chicken broth (3½-cups)**
- 2 **cups sliced carrots**
- 1 **large potato, peeled and diced**
- 1 **cup chopped onion**
- 1 **tablespoon grated fresh ginger**
- ½ **to 1 teaspoon Jamaican jerk seasoning**
- 8 **ounces dried tricolor radiatore or rotini**
- 1½ **cups milk or one 12-ounce can evaporated skim milk**
- **Snipped fresh chives (optional)**

1 In a large saucepan combine chicken broth, carrots, potato, onion, ginger, and Jamaican jerk seasoning. Bring to boiling. Reduce heat and simmer, covered, for 15 to 20 minutes or until vegetables are very tender. Cool slightly.

2 Meanwhile, cook pasta according to package directions; drain.

3 Place one-fourth of the vegetable mixture in a food processor. Cover and process until smooth. Process remaining vegetable mixture one-fourth at a time. Return all to saucepan. Stir in pasta and milk; heat through. Ladle soup into bowls. If desired, sprinkle with chives.

Nutrition Facts per serving: 363 cal., 4 g total fat (2 g sat. fat), 8 mg chol., 750 mg sodium, 65 g carbo., 16 g pro.

Make Ahead: Prepare vegetable mixture and process in food processor as directed. Transfer to a large bowl; cover and chill up to 24 hours. To serve, cook pasta as directed. Transfer vegetable mixture to large saucepan. Stir in pasta and milk; heat through. Continue as directed.

sensational TORTELLINI CHOWDER

Italian-style tortellini combines with Mexican flavors in this hearty chowder. Make it as spicy as you like with green chile and jalapeño peppers.

Prep: 30 minutes
Cook: 26 minutes
Makes: 6 to 8 servings

⅔ **cup chopped onion**

½ **cup chopped red sweet pepper**

⅓ **cup chopped fresh green chile pepper, such as anaheim or poblano***

1 **fresh jalapeño chile pepper, seeded, if desired, and chopped (about 1 tablespoon)***

2 **tablespoons minced garlic**

1 **tablespoon butter or margarine**

3 **cups chicken broth**

2 **cups cubed peeled potatoes**

1 **teaspoon ground cumin**

¼ **teaspoon salt**

¼ **teaspoon ground black pepper**

⅛ **teaspoon cayenne pepper**

2 **tablespoons all-purpose flour**

2 **tablespoons butter or margarine, melted**

1 **15.25-ounce can whole kernel corn, drained**

2 **cups half-and-half or light cream**

2 **cups refrigerated or frozen spinach tortellini, cooked and drained**

Tortilla chips, broken (optional)

1 In a 4- to 6-quart Dutch oven, cook onion, sweet pepper, green chile pepper, jalapeño pepper, and garlic in 1 tablespoon butter about 5 minutes or until vegetables are tender, but not brown.

2 Carefully stir in broth, potatoes, cumin, salt, black pepper, and cayenne pepper. Bring to boiling; reduce heat. Cover and simmer for 25 to 30 minutes or until potatoes are just tender.

3 In a small bowl stir together flour and 2 tablespoons melted butter; add to soup mixture. Cook and stir over medium heat until thickened and bubbly. Cook and stir for 1 minute more.

4 Reduce heat and add corn, half-and-half, and tortellini. Heat through. Ladle into warm soup bowls and, if desired, top with tortilla chips.

Nutrition Facts per serving: 387 cal., 18 g total fat (11 g sat. fat), 64 mg chol., 979 mg sodium, 47 g carbo., 11 g pro.

*Note: Because hot chile peppers contain volatile oils that can burn your skin and eyes, avoid direct contact with chiles as much as possible. When working with chile peppers, wear plastic or rubber gloves. If your bare hands do touch the chile peppers, wash your hands well with soap and water.

pasta SALADS

Italian Basil, Tomato, and Pasta Salad, *recipe page 53*

ginger-chicken PASTA SALAD

The flavors of Asia dominate in this pasta salad. Its fresh and colorful appearance will be a welcome addition to any potluck table.

Prep: 35 minutes
Chill: 4 to 24 hours
Makes: 10 to 12 servings

- 1 **pound dried rotini or small bow ties**
- 3 **cups snow peas, tips and strings removed**
- ⅓ **cup salad oil**
- ⅓ **cup rice vinegar**
- ¼ **cup sugar**
- ¼ **cup soy sauce**
- 1 **tablespoon grated fresh ginger**
- 1 **teaspoon crushed red pepper**
- 1¼ **pounds cooked chicken, cut into bite-size strips (4 cups)**
- 3 **cups yellow and/or red sweet pepper strips**
- 1½ **cups thinly sliced radishes**
- 1 **cup bias-sliced green onions**
- ⅓ **cup snipped fresh cilantro or parsley**
- 1 **cup chopped peanuts**

1 Cook pasta according to package directions; drain. Rinse with cold water; drain again.

2 Meanwhile, cook snow peas in boiling water for 30 seconds. Drain; rinse with cold water. Cover and chill until serving time.

3 For dressing, in a screw-top jar combine oil, vinegar, sugar, soy sauce, ginger, and crushed red pepper. Cover and shake well.

4 In a very large bowl combine cooked pasta, chicken, sweet pepper strips, radishes, green onions, and cilantro. Add dressing; toss gently to coat. Cover and chill for 4 to 24 hours.

5 Just before serving, add pea pods to salad; toss to mix and coat with dressing. Sprinkle salad with peanuts.

Nutrition Facts per serving: 484 cal., 20 g total fat (3 g sat. fat), 50 mg chol., 492 mg sodium, 48 g carbo., 28 g pro.

chicken and grape
PASTA SALAD

Prep: 40 minutes
Chill: 2 hours
Makes: 6 servings

1 2- to 2½-pound deli-roasted chicken or 3 cups chopped cooked chicken

1½ cups dried radiatore, mostaccioli, tirali, and/or medium shell pasta

3 cups assorted fresh grapes, halved and seeded, if necessary

1½ cups halved small strawberries

1 cup chopped peeled jicama or 1 8-ounce can sliced water chestnuts, drained

⅔ cup bottled cucumber ranch salad dressing

⅛ teaspoon cayenne pepper

1 to 2 tablespoons milk (optional)

Leaf lettuce

Purchased sugared sliced almonds (optional)

1 Remove skin and bones from chicken and discard. Tear chicken into bite-size pieces. Cook pasta according to package directions. Drain pasta. Rinse with cold water. Drain again.

2 In a large salad bowl place chicken, pasta, grapes, strawberries, and jicama; toss to combine

3 For dressing, in a small bowl stir together dressing and pepper. Pour dressing over chicken mixture. Toss lightly to coat. Cover and chill for 4 to 24 hours.

4 Before serving, if necessary, stir in enough milk (1 to 2 tablespoons) to moisten. Serve salad on lettuce-lined plates and, if desired, sprinkle with almonds.

Nutrition Facts per serving: 455 cal., 20 g total fat (3 g sat. fat), 67 mg chol., 269 mg sodium, 43 g carbo., 27 g pro.

chicken noodle SALAD WITH PEANUT DRESSING

Prep: 25 minutes
Chill: 4 hours
Makes: 4 servings

¾ **cup water**

¼ **cup peanut butter**

¼ **cup soy sauce**

2 **tablespoons red wine vinegar**

2 **tablespoons olive oil or salad oil**

1 **tablespoon sugar**

1 **tablespoon toasted sesame oil**

1 **tablespoon lemon juice**

1 **teaspoon grated fresh ginger**

1 **clove garlic, minced**

1 **teaspoon chili paste or ½ teaspoon crushed red pepper**

6 **ounces linguine or very thin spaghetti**

2 **cups cooked chicken, cut into strips (10 ounces)**

1 **medium cucumber, halved lengthwise, seeded, and sliced**

1 **cup fresh pea pods, strings removed and bias sliced into ½-inch pieces**

4 **green onions, cut into ½-inch pieces**

1 **medium tomato, chopped**

2 **cups shredded napa cabbage**

2 **cups shredded spinach**

¼ **cup peanuts**

1 In a blender container combine water, peanut butter, soy sauce, red wine vinegar, olive oil, sugar, toasted sesame oil, lemon juice, ginger, garlic, and chili paste. Cover and blend until smooth. Chill up to 24 hours.

2 Cook pasta according to package directions for al dente. Drain; rinse under cold water.

3 In a bowl combine linguine, chicken strips, cucumber, pea pods, green onions, and tomato. Pour the dressing over noodle mixture. Toss gently to mix. Cover and chill chicken mixture for 4 to 24 hours, stirring mixture two or three times.

4 To serve, line four dinner plates or salad plates with the shredded napa cabbage and spinach. Top with chicken mixture. Sprinkle with peanuts.

Nutrition Facts per serving: 620 cal., 30 g total fat (5 g sat. fat), 68 mg chol., 1,139 mg sodium, 53 g carbo., 39 g pro.

grilled chicken and pasta
SALAD WITH CILANTRO PESTO

Prep: 30 minutes
Grill: 12 minutes
Makes: 8 (1½-cup) servings

12 **ounces dried bow tie pasta (4 cups)**

12 **ounces skinless, boneless chicken breast halves**

1 **red sweet pepper, quartered lengthwise and seeded**

1 **green sweet pepper, quartered lengthwise and seeded**

1 **red onion, cut into ½-inch-thick slices**

2 **tablespoons olive oil**

1 **15-ounce can black beans, rinsed and drained**

2 **large tomatoes, chopped**

4 **green onions, thinly sliced**

Cilantro Pesto*

Lime wedges (optional)

Fresh cilantro sprigs (optional)

1 Cook pasta according to package directions; drain. Rinse with cold water; drain again. Place drained pasta in a very large bowl; set aside.

2 Brush chicken, pepper quarters, and onion slices with oil and sprinkle lightly with salt and pepper. For a charcoal grill, place chicken and vegetables on the rack of an uncovered grill directly over medium coals. Grill until chicken is no longer pink (170°F) and vegetables are crisp-tender, turning once halfway through grilling. Allow 12 to 15 minutes for chicken and 8 to 10 minutes for vegetables. (For a gas grill, preheat grill. Reduce heat to medium. Place chicken and vegetables on grill rack over heat. Cover and grill as above.)

3 Remove chicken and vegetables from grill. Chop chicken, sweet peppers, and red onion. Add all to bowl with pasta. Stir in beans, tomatoes, and green onions. Add Cilantro Pesto to pasta mixture; toss gently to coat. Season to taste with salt and pepper. Serve immediately or cover and chill up to 24 hours. If desired, serve with fresh lime wedges and garnish with cilantro sprigs.

***Cilantro Pesto:** In a food processor combine 2 cups fresh cilantro leaves; ⅓ cup olive oil; ½ cup grated Parmesan cheese; ¼ cup pumpkin seeds, shelled sunflower seeds, or toasted pine nuts; 2 cloves garlic; 3 tablespoons lime juice; ¼ teaspoon salt; and several dashes of bottled hot pepper sauce. Cover and process until well combined and nearly smooth, stopping and scraping down sides of bowl as necessary. Makes about 1 cup.

Nutrition Facts per serving: 421 cal., 17 g total fat (3 g sat. fat), 29 mg chol., 317 mg sodium, 46 g carbo., 23 g pro.

turkey AND PASTA SALAD

This delicious version of a Waldorf salad builds on the classic, but goes modern with smoked turkey, raspberries, and curly rotini pasta—and lightens up with a low-fat dressing.

Start to Finish: 25 minutes
Makes: 4 servings

- 6 **ounces dried rotini or radiatore**
- 1 **medium apple, chopped**
- 1 **tablespoon lime or lemon juice**
- ½ **pound smoked turkey breast, cut into bite-size pieces**
- 1 **cup raspberries or strawberries, cut in quarters**
- ½ **cup sliced celery**
- ¼ **cup plain fat-free yogurt**
- 2 **tablespoons fat-free mayonnaise or salad dressing**
- 2 **tablespoons skim milk**
- 4 **teaspoons Dijon-style mustard**
- 1 **tablespoon snipped fresh marjoram**
- ¼ **teaspoon celery seeds**

1 Cook pasta according to package directions; drain. Rinse with cold water; drain again.

2 Toss chopped apple with lime juice. In a large mixing bowl combine pasta, chopped apple, turkey, raspberries, and celery.

3 For dressing, in a small mixing bowl combine yogurt, mayonnaise, milk, mustard, marjoram, and celery seeds. Drizzle dressing over pasta mixture; toss gently to coat.

Nutrition Facts per serving: 278 cal., 2 g total fat (0 g sat. fat), 25 mg chol., 820 mg sodium, 45 g carbo., 19 g pro.

smoked turkey AND
TORTELLINI SALAD

Start to Finish: 25 minutes
Makes: 4 servings

1   **7- to 8-ounce package dried cheese-filled tortellini**

1   **cup chopped, cooked smoked turkey, ham, or chicken**

8   **cherry tomatoes, quartered**

½   **cup coarsely chopped green sweet pepper**

¼   **cup sliced pitted ripe olives (optional)**

¼   **cup bottled Italian vinaigrette or balsamic vinaigrette salad dressing**

Black pepper

1 Cook tortellini according to package directions; drain. Rinse with cold water; drain again.

2 In a large bowl combine tortellini, turkey, tomatoes, sweet pepper, and, if desired, olives. Drizzle salad dressing over mixture; toss to coat. Season to taste with pepper. Serve immediately.

Nutrition Facts per serving: 330 cal., 15 g total fat (2 g sat. fat), 20 mg chol., 897 mg sodium, 32 g carbo., 17 g pro.

beefy PASTA SALAD

Start to Finish: 30 minutes
Makes: 4 (1⅓ cup) servings

1 cup dried multigrain penne
   pasta (about 3½ ounces)

2 ears of corn, husks and silks
   removed

   Nonstick cooking spray

12 ounces boneless beef sirloin
    steak, trimmed of fat, cut
    into thin bite-size strips, or
    2 cups shredded cooked
    beef pot roast (10 ounces)*

1 cup cherry tomatoes, halved

¼ cup shredded fresh basil

2 tablespoons finely shredded
   Parmesan cheese

3 tablespoons white wine
   vinegar

1 tablespoon olive oil

1 clove garlic, minced

¼ teaspoon salt

⅛ teaspoon ground black
   pepper

¼ cup finely shredded Parmesan
   cheese

1 In a 4- to 6-quart Dutch oven, cook pasta according to package directions, adding corn for the last 3 minutes of cooking time. Using tongs, transfer corn to a large cutting board. Drain pasta. Rinse in cold water and drain again; set aside. Cool corn until easy to handle.

2 Meanwhile, coat an unheated large nonstick skillet with cooking spray. Preheat skillet over medium-high heat. Add beef strips. Cook for 4 to 6 minutes or until slightly pink in the center, stirring occasionally. (If using shredded beef, cook until heated through.) Remove from heat and cool slightly.

3 On a cutting board, place an ear of corn pointed end down. While holding corn firmly at stem end to keep in place, use a sharp knife to cut corn from cobs, leaving corn in planks; rotate cob as needed to cut corn from all sides. Repeat with the remaining ear of corn. In a large bowl combine pasta, beef, tomatoes, basil, and the 2 tablespoons Parmesan cheese.

4 In a screw-top jar combine vinegar, oil, garlic, salt, and pepper. Cover and shake well. Pour over pasta mixture; toss gently to coat. Gently fold in corn planks or place corn planks on top of individual servings. Serve immediately. Garnish with ¼ cup Parmesan cheese.

Nutrition Facts per serving: 313 cal., 10 g total fat (3 g sat. fat), 41 mg chol., 341 mg sodium, 28 g carbo., 28 g pro.

*Test Kitchen Tip: If you have leftover beef pot roast, simply shred the meat and use 2 cups of it in the salad.

grilled steak AND PASTA SALAD

Prep: 15 minutes
Chill: 1 hour
Cook: 10 minutes
Grill: 10 minutes
Makes: 6 servings

¼ **cup rice vinegar**

2 **tablespoons light mayonnaise**

2 **tablespoons extra-virgin olive oil**

1 **teaspoon salt**

½ **teaspoon dried oregano**

½ **teaspoon ground cumin**

¼ **teaspoon cayenne pepper**

12 **ounces flank steak**

½ **teaspoon Montreal steak seasoning**

½ **pound bow tie pasta**

2 **large tomatoes, cut into 1-inch pieces**

1 **medium-size sweet onion, quartered and thinly sliced**

2 **cups corn kernels from 2 ears of corn**

⅓ **cup fresh flat-leaf parsley, chopped**

⅓ **cup fresh basil, chopped**

8 **cups mixed salad greens**

1 In a bowl whisk vinegar, mayonnaise, oil, salt, oregano, cumin, and cayenne until well blended. Set aside.

2 Heat a gas grill to medium-high or prepare a grill with medium-hot coals. Bring a large pot of water to a boil.

3 Sprinkle steak with the seasoning. Grill 4 to 5 minutes per side or until internal temperature reads 145°F on an instant-read thermometer for medium-rare. Let rest 10 minutes then cut into thin slices.

4 Cook pasta in boiling water. Drain; rinse under cold water.

5 Toss pasta with dressing in serving bowl. Add steak, tomatoes, onion, corn, parsley, and basil to bowl; toss to combine. Chill 1 hour, then serve over greens.

Nutrition Facts per serving: 328 cal., 12 g total fat (3 g sat. fat), 25 mg chol., 605 mg sodium, 39 g carbo., 19 g pro.

spicy beef AND NOODLE SALAD

Let the steak rest for 5 or 10 minutes before slicing it. Just that few minutes allows the juices to be absorbed back into the meat so they don't wind up on your cutting board.

Start to Finish: 20 minutes
Makes: 4 servings

1   **pound beef flank steak**

1   **tablespoon soy sauce**

8   **ounces rice noodles**

1   **medium English cucumber**

½   **cup Asian sweet chili sauce**

½   **cup water**

1   **cup packaged fresh julienned carrots**

Fresh cilantro leaves (optional)

1 Preheat broiler. Trim fat from steak. Brush steak with soy sauce. Place steak on the rack of an unheated broiler pan. Broil 4 to 5 inches from heat for 15 to 18 minutes or to desired doneness (160°F for medium), turning once halfway through broiling. Thinly slice beef across the grain.

2 Meanwhile, cook noodles according to package directions; drain in colander. Rinse with cold water.

3 Slice cucumber crosswise in three sections. Using a vegetable peeler, cut lengthwise ribbons from sections.

4 In a small bowl combine chili sauce and water. Divide steak, noodles, cucumber, and carrots among four bowls. Drizzle with chili sauce mixture. If desired, garnish with cilantro.

Nutrition Facts per serving: 477 cal., 9 g total fat (4 g sat. fat), 40 mg chol., 839 mg sodium, 70 g carbo., 27 g pro.

wheelie HAM SALAD

Serve up this pasta salad loaded with summer zucchini, savory ham, and juicy tomatoes.

Prep: 25 minutes
Chill: 2 to 24 hours
Makes: 4 main-dish servings

4   ounces dried wagon wheel
     pasta (1½ cups)

4   ounces cooked lean ham, cut
     into bite-size pieces

1   small zucchini, quartered
     lengthwise and sliced

2   tablespoons sliced green
     onion (optional)

⅓   cup bottled reduced-fat ranch
     salad dressing

2   tablespoons plain low-fat
     yogurt

1   teaspoon dried basil, crushed

¾   cup grape or cherry
     tomatoes, halved

1 In a large saucepan cook pasta according to package directions. Drain. Rinse with cold water. Drain again. In a large bowl combine cooked pasta, ham, zucchini, and, if desired, green onion.

2 For dressing, in a small bowl stir together salad dressing, yogurt, and basil. Pour dressing over pasta mixture. Toss lightly to coat. Cover and chill for 2 to 24 hours. Before serving, gently stir tomatoes into pasta mixture.

Nutrition Facts per serving: 214 cal., 8 g total fat (1 g sat. fat), 23 mg chol., 596 mg sodium, 27 g carbo., 10 g pro.

asian-style PORK AND NOODLE SALAD

Look for bottled Thai peanut sauce in your supermarket's Asian foods section or at an Asian market.

Prep: 30 minutes
Broil: 9 minutes
Chill: 4 hours
Makes: 5 servings

1   3-ounce package pork- or chicken-flavor ramen noodles

½   **cup salad oil**

⅓   **cup rice vinegar**

3   **cloves garlic, minced**

3   **tablespoons Thai peanut sauce**

¼   **teaspoon crushed red pepper**

12   **ounces boneless pork loin chops, cut ¾-inch thick**

4   **cups shredded cabbage**

1   **cup broccoli florets**

½   **cup sliced almonds, toasted**

½   **cup sliced green onions**

1 Measure out ¾ teaspoon of the seasoning packet (half of the packet); reserve the remaining for another use. In a medium bowl whisk together the ¾ teaspoon seasoning, salad oil, rice vinegar, garlic, peanut sauce, and red pepper. Remove 2 tablespoons of the mixture; brush onto pork chops.

2 Preheat broiler. Place pork on the unheated rack of a broiler pan. Broil 3 to 4 inches from the heat for 9 to 12 minutes or until meat juices run clear (160°F), turning chops once. Cool slightly. Thinly slice across the grain into bite-size strips.

3 Meanwhile, cook noodles in a large saucepan in boiling water for 2 minutes drain. Transfer to a large bowl. Add the pork, cabbage, broccoli, almonds, green onions, and remaining oil mixture. Toss to coat. Cover and chill for 4 to 24 hours.

4 To tote, spoon into five individual containers; pack each with an ice pick. Eat within 5 hours.

Nutrition Facts per serving: 505 cal., 38 g total fat (6 g sat. fat), 40 mg chol., 490 mg sodium, 22 g carbo., 22 g pro.

italian basil, TOMATO, AND PASTA SALAD

Prep: 45 minutes
Chill: 4 to 24 hours
Makes: 16 side-dish servings

½ **cup red wine vinegar**

2 **tablespoons Dijon-style mustard**

2 **cloves garlic, minced**

½ **cup olive oil**

½ **cup slivered fresh basil**

8 **ounces dried pasta (such as rotini, bow ties, shells, cavatelli, or penne)**

1 **lb. fresh green beans, cut up, or two 9-ounce pkg. frozen cut green beans (about 4 cups)**

6 **medium tomatoes, cut into thin wedges (about 2 pounds)**

1 **cup sliced, pitted kalamata olives or ripe olives**

2 **cups loosely packed fresh basil leaves**

¾ **cup finely shredded Parmesan cheese (3 ounces)**

3 **tablespoons snipped fresh parsley**

1 For dressing, in a small bowl whisk together vinegar, mustard, garlic, and ¼ teaspoon pepper. Gradually whisk in oil; set aside.

2 Cook pasta according to package directions; drain. Rinse with cold water; drain again.

3 Meanwhile, in covered large saucepan cook fresh green beans in a moderate amount of boiling water for 9 to 12 minutes or until crisp-tender. (Or cook frozen beans according to package directions.) Drain.

4 Toss one-third of the dressing (about ⅓ cup) with the drained pasta. Place pasta mixture in the bottom of a large (about 4-quart) salad bowl. Layer green beans, tomatoes, and olives on top. Add the ½ cup slivered basil to remaining dressing; pour over ingredients in salad bowl. Sprinkle with the 2 cups whole basil leaves, the cheese, and parsley. Cover tightly with plastic wrap. Refrigerate for at least 4 hours or up to 24 hours. To serve, toss lightly.

Nutrition Facts per serving: 175 cal., 10 g total fat (2 g sat. fat), 5 mg chol., 170 mg sodium, 17 g carbo., 5 g pro.

citrus tuna PASTA SALAD

Yellow sweet peppers, artichoke hearts, ripe olives, and a light lemon-herb dressing highlight this delicious pasta salad.

Prep: 30 minutes
Chill: 1 hour
Makes: 4 main-dish servings

- 6 ounces dried mafalda pasta or medium shell macaroni
- 1 9-ounce package frozen artichoke hearts, thawed
- 1 9¼-ounce can chunk white tuna (water pack), drained and broken into chunks
- 1 cup sliced fresh mushrooms
- 1 cup chopped yellow sweet pepper
- ¼ cup sliced pitted ripe olives
  Lemon Dressing*
- 1 cup cherry tomatoes, halved
- 2 tablespoons finely shredded Parmesan cheese

1 Cook pasta according to package directions, except omit any oil or salt. Add artichoke hearts to pasta the last 5 minutes of cooking. Drain in colander. Rinse with cold water; drain again. Halve any large artichoke hearts.

2 Transfer pasta mixture to a large bowl. Gently stir in tuna, mushrooms, sweet pepper, and olives. Prepare Lemon Dressing. Pour dressing over pasta mixture; toss to coat. Cover; refrigerate for at least 1 hour. Gently stir in tomatoes. Sprinkle with Parmesan cheese.

*Lemon Dressing: In a small bowl whisk together 1 teaspoon finely shredded lemon peel; 3 tablespoons lemon juice; 3 tablespoons rice vinegar or white wine vinegar; 2 tablespoons salad oil; 1 tablespoon snipped fresh thyme or basil or 1 teaspoon dried thyme or basil, crushed; 2 cloves garlic; ½ teaspoon sugar; and ¼ teaspoon black pepper.

Nutrition Facts per serving: 389 cal., 11 g total fat (1 g sat. fat), 22 mg chol., 369 mg sodium, 49 g carbo., 27 g pro.

greek PASTA SALAD

The fresh herbs, vegetables, and olives that characterize Greek cuisine are tossed with pasta in this sprightly salad. Feta cheese gives it a tangy finish.

Prep: 40 minutes
Chill: 2 to 24 hours
Makes: 12 to 16 side-dish servings

12 ounces dried mostaccioli or penne (about 4 cups uncooked)

2 cups cherry tomatoes, quartered

1 medium cucumber, halved lengthwise and sliced

4 green onions, sliced

⅓ cup pitted kalamata olives, halved

½ cup olive oil

½ cup lemon juice

2 tablespoons snipped fresh basil or 2 teaspoons dried basil, crushed

2 tablespoons snipped fresh oregano or 2 teaspoons dried oregano, crushed

1 tablespoon anchovy paste (optional)

4 to 6 cloves garlic, minced

¼ teaspoon salt

¼ teaspoon ground black pepper

1 cup crumbled feta cheese (4 ounces)

Fresh oregano leaves

1 Cook pasta according to package directions. Drain in a colander. Rinse with cold water; drain again.

2 In a large bowl toss together the cooked pasta, tomatoes, cucumber, green onions, and olives.

3 In a screw-top jar combine the olive oil, lemon juice, basil, the 2 tablespoons oregano, anchovy paste (if using), garlic, salt, and pepper. Cover and shake well. Drizzle over past mixture; toss to coat.

4 Cover and chill in refrigerator for as least 2 hours or up to 24 hours. To serve, add feta cheese; toss. Sprinkle fresh oregano leaves.

Nutrition Facts per serving: 231 cal., 12 g total fat (3 g sat. fat), 8 mg chol., 200 mg sodium, 26 g carbo., 6 g pro.

ravioli AND GREENS SALAD

Start to Finish: 25 minutes
Makes: 4 servings

1   9-ounce package refrigerated whole wheat four cheese ravioli

6   cups torn mixed greens

1   medium red pepper, cut into bite-size strips

1   medium yellow and/or red tomato, cut into wedges

¼   cup shredded carrot

¼   cup snipped fresh basil, oregano, and/or dill

¼   cup white wine vinegar or white vinegar

2   tablespoons water

2   tablespoons olive oil

2   teaspoons sugar

2   cloves garlic, minced

¼   teaspoon ground black pepper

1 In a large saucepan cook ravioli according to package directions, except omit oil and salt; drain. Rinse with cold water; drain.

2 Arrange greens on four dinner plates. Top with cooked ravioli, red pepper, tomato, carrot, and herbs.

3 For dressing, in a screw-top jar combine white wine vinegar, water, oil, sugar, garlic, and black pepper. Cover and shake well. Drizzle over salads.

Nutrition Facts per about 2 cups salad and 2 tablespoons dressing: 302 cal., 14 g total fat (5 g sat. fat), 43 mg chol., 456 mg sodium, 33 g carbo., 11 g pro.

Money-Saving Tip: Use canned tomatoes rather than fresh, but make sure to rinse them well or get the no-salt-added kind to keep from adding any sodium to the salad.

penne salad WITH GREEN BEANS AND GORGONZOLA

Start to Finish: 25 minutes
Makes: 8 servings

- 6 ounces dried penne or cut ziti pasta
- 8 ounces fresh green beans, trimmed and bias-sliced into 1-inch pieces (about 1½ cups), or one 9-ounce package frozen cut green beans, thawed
- ⅓ cup bottled Italian salad dressing
- 1 tablespoon snipped fresh tarragon or ½ teaspoon dried tarragon, crushed
- ¼ teaspoon ground black pepper
- 1 cup shredded radicchio or red cabbage
- 1 6-ounce package fresh baby spinach
- ½ cup crumbled Gorgonzola cheese or blue cheese (2 ounces) or ¼ cup shaved Parmesan cheese (1 ounce)

1 Cook pasta according to package directions, adding fresh green beans during the last 5 to 7 minutes of cooking (if using frozen beans, add during the last 3 to 4 minutes); drain. Rinse with cold water; drain again.

2 In a large bowl combine Italian dressing, tarragon, and pepper. Add cooked pasta mixture and radicchio; toss gently to coat. Line a serving platter with spinach. Spoon pasta mixture on top of spinach. Sprinkle with cheese.

Nutrition Facts per serving: 147 cal., 5 g total fat (2 g sat. fat), 5 mg chol., 280 mg sodium, 20 g carbo., 6 g pro.

pea and macaroni SALAD

It's not necessary to allow the macaroni to cool before mixing with the dressing. Once it's chilled, you can stir in additional milk to moisten the salad.

Prep: 20 minutes
Chill: 4 hours
Makes: 12 to 16 side-dish
     servings

1 **cup fresh pea pods**

8 **ounces dried elbow macaroni**

1 **cup frozen peas, thawed**

½ **cup mayonnaise or salad
   dressing**

½ **cup dairy sour cream**

⅓ **cup milk**

¼ **cup horseradish mustard**

2 **cloves garlic, minced**

¼ **teaspoon salt**

¼ **teaspoon pepper**

¾ **cup thinly sliced celery**

2 **tablespoons chopped onion**

  Milk (optional)

  Pea pods (optional)

1 Remove tips and strings from pea pods. Cook macaroni according to package directions in lightly salted boiling water, adding pea pods and peas during the last 1 minute of cooking. Drain and rinse. Halve pea pods diagonally; set macaroni, pea pods, and peas aside.

2 In a small bowl stir together mayonnaise, sour cream, milk, mustard, minced garlic, salt, and pepper; set aside.

3 In a large bowl combine cooked macaroni mixture, celery, and onion. Pour mayonnaise mixture over the macaroni mixture. Stir gently to combine.

4 Cover and chill 4 to 24 hours. Stir mixture before serving. If necessary, add additional milk (1 to 2 tablespoons) to moisten. If desired, top with additional pea pods.

Nutrition Facts per serving: 178 cal., 10 g total fat (2 g sat. fat), 7 mg chol., 169 mg sodium, 18 g carbo., 4 g pro.

baked
PASTA DISHES

Cheesy Chicken and Mostaccioli,
recipe page 71

20-minute chicken
MAC AND CHEESE

Spiffed up with chicken, Italian seasoning, smoked cheddar cheese, and sourdough bread crumbs, this tomatoey version of mac and cheese is more at home at a bistro than a diner.

Prep: 40 minutes
Bake: 20 minutes
Stand: 10 minutes
Makes: 6 servings

- 1 **tablespoon olive oil**
- 1 **pound skinless, boneless chicken breasts, cut into bite-size pieces**
- 1 **to 2 teaspoons dried Italian seasoning, crushed**
  Salt
  Black pepper
- 8 **ounces dried mostaccioli, ziti, or penne pasta**
- 3 **tablespoons butter**
- 1 **medium onion, chopped**
- 2 **cloves garlic, minced**
- 3 **tablespoons all-purpose flour**
- 2 **tablespoons tomato paste**
- 3 **cups milk**
- 8 **ounces smoked cheddar, Gruyère, or Swiss cheese, shredded (2 cups)**
- 2 **cups soft sourdough or French bread crumbs**
- ½ **cup finely shredded Parmesan or Romano cheese (2 ounces)**
- 3 **tablespoons butter, melted**

1 Preheat oven to 350°F. In a large skillet heat oil over medium heat. Add chicken, Italian seasoning, ⅛ teaspoon salt, and ⅛ teaspoon pepper; cook until chicken is tender and no longer pink. Remove chicken from skillet; set aside.

2 Cook pasta according to package directions just until tender. Drain; return pasta to hot pan.

3 Meanwhile, in same skillet melt 3 tablespoons butter over medium heat. Add onion and garlic; cook until tender. Stir in flour. Stir in tomato paste. Add milk. Cook and stir until mixture is thickened and bubbly; reduce heat. Add shredded smoked cheddar cheese, stirring until cheese is almost melted. Remove from heat; season to taste with additional salt and pepper. Add cheese mixture and chicken to cooked pasta, stirring to coat. Spoon mixture into a 2-quart square or rectangular baking dish. In a small bowl stir together bread crumbs, Parmesan cheese, and 3 tablespoons melted butter.

4 Preheat oven to 350°F. Sprinkle crumb mixture over pasta mixture. Bake for 20 to 25 minutes or until crumb mixture is golden and edges are bubbly. Let stand for 10 minutes before serving.

Nutrition Facts per serving: 670 cal., 33 g total fat (19 g sat. fat), 131 mg chol., 710 mg sodium, 49 g carbo., 42 g pro.

creamy chicken AND
TOMATO PASTA

Chicken noodle casserole is updated with dried tomatoes, fresh basil, and creamy Alfredo sauce.

Prep: 25 minutes
Bake: 25 minutes
Oven: 350°F
Makes: 6 servings

8 ounces pasta (such as linguine, bow tie, penne, or rotelle)

2 shallots, chopped

1 clove garlic, minced

1 tablespoon olive oil

12 ounces skinless, boneless chicken breast halves, cut into bite-size pieces

¼ cup dry white wine or chicken broth

¼ cup snipped fresh basil

1 tablespoon snipped Italian parsley

1 10-ounce container refrigerated light Alfredo sauce

¾ cup oil-pack dried tomatoes, drained and thinly sliced

⅓ cup milk

½ cup grated Parmesan cheese

¼ teaspoon pepper

Fresh basil (optional)

1 Cook pasta according to package directions; drain. Meanwhile, in a large skillet cook shallots and garlic in hot olive oil over medium-high heat for 30 seconds. Add chicken. Cook and stir for 3 to 4 minutes or until chicken is no longer pink. Drain fat. Carefully add wine, snipped basil, and parsley. Cook for 1 minute more.

2 In a large mixing bowl combine cooked pasta, chicken mixture, Alfredo sauce, dried tomatoes, milk, ¼ cup of the Parmesan cheese, and pepper.

3 Transfer to a 2-quart rectangular baking dish. Sprinkle with remaining Parmesan cheese. Cover and bake in a 350°F oven for 15 minutes. Uncover and bake for 10 to 15 minutes more or until heated through and top is slightly golden. Garnish with fresh basil, if desired.

Nutrition Facts per serving: 428 cal., 16 g total fat (7 g sat. fat), 58 mg chol., 640 mg sodium, 45 g carbo., 24 g pro.

Make Ahead: Prepare casserole except do not bake. Cover with foil and chill up to 24 hours. Bake in a 350°F oven for 25 minutes. Uncover and bake for 10 to 15 minutes more or until heated through and top is slightly golden.

tortellini and garden
VEGETABLE BAKE

Use refrigerated or dried tortellini for this chicken and pasta bake.

Prep: 30 minutes
Bake: 30 minutes
Makes: 12 main-dish servings

10 ounces dried cheese-filled tortellini (2½ cups) or two 9-ounce packages refrigerated tortellini

1 medium carrot, thinly sliced

1½ cups sugar snap peas, halved crosswise

1 tablespoon margarine or butter

1 pound skinless, boneless chicken breasts, cut into bite-size pieces

1 cup sliced fresh mushrooms

⅓ cup chicken broth

2 tablespoons snipped fresh oregano or 1½ teaspoons dried oregano, crushed

2 teaspoons all-purpose flour

¾ teaspoon garlic salt

½ teaspoon pepper

1 cup milk

1 8-ounce package cream cheese or light cream cheese (Neufchatel), cubed and softened

1 tablespoon lemon juice

1 cup quartered cherry tomatoes

1 small red or green sweet pepper, coarsely chopped

2 tablespoons grated Parmesan cheese

❶ Cook tortellini in boiling salted water according to package directions, adding the carrot during the last 5 minutes of cooking and the sugar snap peas during the last 1 minute of cooking; drain.

❷ Meanwhile, heat margarine in a 12-inch skillet. Add chicken and mushrooms, and cook about 5 minutes or until chicken is no longer pink. Remove from skillet.

❸ Shake together chicken broth, oregano, flour, garlic salt, and pepper in a screw-top jar until smooth. Add to skillet along with milk. Cook and stir until thickened and bubbly; add cream cheese. Cook and stir until cream cheese is smooth. Remove from heat. Stir in lemon juice. Add pasta mixture, chicken mixture, tomatoes, and sweet pepper. Toss to coat. Turn into an ungreased shallow 3-quart baking dish.

❹ Bake, covered, in a 350°F oven for 30 to 35 minutes or until heated through. Stir mixture and sprinkle with Parmesan cheese.

Nutrition Facts per serving: 247 cal., 12 g total fat (5 g sat. fat), 43 mg chol., 477 mg sodium, 17 g carbo., 15 g pro.

Make Ahead: Prepare as directed but don't bake it. Instead, cover and chill up to 24 hours. Bake, covered, in a 350°F oven about 55 minutes or until hot.

chicken florentine
ARTICHOKE BAKE

Prep: 30 minutes
Bake: 30 minutes
Oven: 350°F
Makes: 6 to 8 servings

- 8 ounces dried bow tie pasta
- 1 small onion, chopped
- 1 Tbsp. butter
- 2 eggs
- 1¼ cups milk
- 1 teaspoon dried Italian seasoning
- ¼ to ½ teaspoon crushed red pepper (optional)
- 2 cups chopped cooked chicken
- 2 cups shredded Monterey Jack cheese (8 oz.)
- 1 14-oz. can artichoke hearts, drained and quartered
- 1 10-oz. pkg. frozen chopped spinach, thawed and well drained
- ½ cup oil-packed dried tomatoes, drained and chopped
- ¼ cup grated Parmesan cheese
- ½ cup soft bread crumbs
- ½ teaspoon paprika
- 1 tablespoon butter, melted

1 Preheat oven to 350°F. Cook pasta according to package directions; drain. In medium skillet cook onion in 1 tablespoon butter over medium heat about 5 minutes or until tender, stirring occasionally. Remove from heat; set aside.

2 In a bowl whisk together eggs, milk, seasoning, ½ teaspoon salt, ¼ teaspoon black pepper, and crushed red pepper. Stir in chicken, Monterey Jack cheese, artichokes, spinach, tomatoes, half of the Parmesan, cooked pasta, and onion. Transfer to 3-quart rectangular baking dish.

3 Bake, covered, 20 minutes. In small bowl combine remaining Parmesan, bread crumbs, paprika, and melted butter. Sprinkle mixture over pasta. Bake, uncovered, 10 minutes more or until golden.

Nutrition Facts per serving: 531 cal., 24 g total fat (13 g sat. fat), 163 mg chol., 897 mg sodium, 41 g carbo., 36 g pro.

shortcut chicken MANICOTTI

To streamline the preparation of this popular pasta casserole, omit cooking the manicotti shells in boiling water. Instead, spoon the filling into uncooked shells—they'll cook as they bake.

Prep: 25 minutes
Bake: 1 hour
Stand: 10 minutes
Makes: 6 servings

- 1 **egg**
- 1 **10-ounce package frozen chopped spinach, thawed and well drained**
- 1 **cup finely chopped cooked chicken or turkey (about 5 ounces)**
- ½ **cup ricotta cheese or cream-style cottage cheese, drained**
- ½ **cup grated Parmesan cheese (2 ounces)**
- 12 **dried manicotti shells**
- 1 **10.75-ounce can condensed cream of chicken soup**
- 1 **8-ounce carton dairy sour cream**
- 1 **cup milk**
- ½ **teaspoon dried Italian seasoning, crushed**
- 1 **cup boiling water**
- 1 **cup shredded mozzarella cheese (4 ounces)**
- 2 **tablespoons snipped fresh parsley (optional)**

1 For filling, in a medium bowl beat egg with a fork; stir in spinach, chicken, ricotta cheese, and Parmesan cheese. Spoon about ¼ cup of the filling into each uncooked manicotti shell. Arrange filled shells in an ungreased 3-quart rectangular baking dish, making sure shells do not touch each other.

2 For sauce, in another medium bowl combine cream of chicken soup, sour cream, milk, and Italian seasoning. Pour over manicotti shells, spreading to cover shells. Slowly pour boiling water around edge of baking dish. Cover baking dish tightly with foil.

3 Bake in a 350°F oven for 60 to 65 minutes or until manicotti shells are tender. Sprinkle with mozzarella cheese and, if desired, parsley. Let stand for 10 minutes before serving.

Nutrition Facts per serving: 463 cal., 23 g total fat (13 g sat. fat), 106 mg chol., 758 mg sodium, 35 g carbo., 27 g pro.

cheesy chicken AND MOSTACCIOLI

Next time you cook chicken for dinner, plan for extra to use in this snazzy pasta and chicken casserole.

Prep: 30 minutes
Bake: 25 minutes
Stand: 10 minutes
Makes: 6 servings

1 **6-ounce package dried mostaccioli with tomato, red pepper, and basil, or plain mostaccioli**

2 **cups loose-pack frozen mixed vegetables**

1 **medium onion, chopped (½ cup)**

2 **tablespoons margarine or butter**

2 **tablespoons all-purpose flour**

2 **teaspoons instant chicken bouillon granules**

2 **cups milk**

1½ **cups shredded Monterey Jack cheese with jalapeno peppers (6 ounces)**

2 **tablespoons snipped fresh cilantro or parsley**

1½ **cups chopped cooked chicken (about 8 ounces) or 1 9.25-ounce can tuna, drained and broken into chunks**

1 **medium tomato, halved and sliced**

1 In a large saucepan or Dutch oven bring about 3 quarts water to boiling. Add pasta. Return to boiling; cook for 9 minutes. Add frozen mixed vegetables. Return to boiling; cook for 5 to 7 minutes more or until pasta is tender but slightly firm and vegetables are crisp-tender. Drain; rinse with cold water. Drain again.

2 For sauce, in a large saucepan cook onion in margarine until tender. Stir in flour and bouillon granules. Add milk all at once. Cook and stir until thickened and bubbly. Add cheese, stirring until melted. Stir in cilantro. Remove from heat.

3 Add pasta and chicken to the sauce; toss to coat. Spoon mixture into a 2-quart square baking dish. Cover dish with foil.

4 Bake in a 375°F oven for 20 minutes. Remove foil from dish. Arrange tomato slices on top of pasta mixture. Bake, uncovered, for 5 to 10 minutes more or until heated through. Let stand 10 minutes before serving.

Nutrition Facts per serving: 417 cal., 18 g total fat (8 g sat. fat), 65 mg chol., 582 mg sodium, 38 g carbo., 27 g pro.

chicken TETRAZZINI

Prep: 30 minutes
Bake: 10 minutes
Oven: 400°F
Makes: 4 servings

6 **ounces dried spaghetti**

1½ **cups sliced fresh mushrooms**

¾ **cup chopped red or green
   sweet pepper**

½ **cup cold water**

¼ **cup all-purpose flour**

1 **12-ounce can (1½ cups)
   evaporated low-fat milk**

1 **teaspoon instant chicken
   bouillon granules**

¼ **teaspoon black pepper**

⅛ **teaspoon salt**

1 **cup chopped cooked chicken
   or turkey (5 ounces)**

¼ **cup finely shredded Parmesan
   cheese (1 ounce)**

2 **tablespoons dry sherry
   or milk**

Nonstick cooking spray

1 **tablespoon sliced almonds**

1 Cook the spaghetti according to package directions, except omit the cooking oil and lightly salt the water. Drain well.

2 Meanwhile, in a large covered saucepan cook the mushrooms and sweet pepper in a small amount of boiling water about 3 minutes or until the vegetables until tender. Drain well; return to saucepan.

3 In a screw-top jar combine ½ cup cold water and flour; cover and shake well. Stir into the vegetable mixture in saucepan. Stir in the evaporated milk, bouillon granules, black pepper, and salt. Cook and stir until thickened and bubbly. Stir in the cooked spaghetti, chicken, Parmesan cheese, and dry sherry.

4 Lightly coat a 2-quart square baking dish with nonstick cooking spray. Spoon spaghetti mixture into dish. Sprinkle with almonds. Bake, uncovered, in a 400°F oven about 10 minutes or until heated through and nuts are lightly toasted.

Nutrition Facts per serving: 394 cal., 9 g total fat (4 g sat. fat), 44 mg chol., 492 mg sodium, 50 g carb., 2 g fiber, 26 g pro.

chicken supreme CASSEROLE

Prep: 30 minutes
Cook: 10 minutes
Bake: 40 minutes
Stand: 10 minutes
Oven: 350°F
Makes: 4 servings

6 cups water

1⅓ cups dried bow tie or rotini pasta (6 ounces)

1 16-ounce package frozen pepper stir-fry vegetables

1 10.75-ounce can reduced-fat and reduced-sodium condensed cream of chicken soup

1¼ cups fat-free milk

3 tablespoons light mayonnaise

1 teaspoon salt-free lemon-pepper seasoning

1 cup cubed cooked chicken breast (6 ounces)

¼ cup sliced green onions

1 Preheat oven to 350°F. In a large saucepan bring the water to boiling. Add pasta; reduce heat. Simmer, uncovered, for 6 minutes, stirring occasionally. Stir in frozen vegetables. Return to boiling; reduce heat. Simmer, uncovered, for 3 to 5 minutes more or until pasta is tender but still firm (al dente); drain. Rinse with cold water; drain again. Set aside.

2 In a large bowl stir together soup, milk, mayonnaise, and lemon-pepper seasoning. Stir in chicken and pasta mixture. Transfer pasta mixture to a 2-quart square baking dish.

3 Cover and bake for 30 minutes; stir. Bake, uncovered, for 10 to 15 minutes more or until mixture is heated through and bubbly. Let stand for 10 minutes before serving. Sprinkle individual servings with green onions.

Nutrition Facts per serving: 359 cal., 7 g total fat (1 g sat. fat), 40 mg chol., 441 mg sodium, 51 g carbo., 22 g pro.

beef stroganoff CASSEROLE

Prep: 35 minutes
Bake: 30 minutes
Oven: 350°F
Makes: 6 servings

12 ounces dried campanelle or
    penne pasta

1 17-ounce package
    refrigerated cooked beef
    roast au jus

2 large fresh portobello
    mushrooms, stems removed
    and coarsely chopped (about
    4 cups)

1 medium sweet onion, cut into
    thin wedges

2 cloves garlic, minced

2 tablespoons butter

3 tablespoons all-purpose flour

2 tablespoons tomato paste

1 14-ounce can beef broth

1 tablespoon Worcestershire
    sauce

1 teaspoon smoked paprika or
    Spanish paprika

¼ teaspoon salt

¼ teaspoon ground black
    pepper

1 8-ounce carton sour cream

1 tablespoon prepared
    horseradish

1 teaspoon snipped fresh dill or
    ¼ teaspoon dried dill

    Fresh dill sprigs (optional)

1 Preheat oven to 350°F. Cook pasta according to package directions; drain. Return to pan.

2 Meanwhile, remove meat from container, reserving juices. Using two forks, shred meat into bite-size pieces. Set aside.

3 In a large skillet cook mushrooms, onion, and garlic in hot butter over medium heat for 4 to 5 minutes or until tender. Stir in flour and tomato paste. Gradually stir in meat juices, broth, Worcestershire sauce, paprika, salt, and pepper. Cook and stir until thickened and bubbly. Remove from heat. Stir in ½ cup of the sour cream.

4 Stir shredded meat and mushroom mixture into cooked pasta. Transfer mixture to an ungreased 3-quart casserole. Bake, covered, about 30 minutes or until heated through.

5 Meanwhile, in a small bowl combine the remaining sour cream, horseradish, and snipped dill. Serve with meat mixture. If desired, garnish with dill sprigs.

Nutrition Facts per serving: 485 cal., 18 g total fat (10 g sat. fat), 72 mg chol., 770 mg sodium, 56 g carbo., 26 g pro.

spaghetti PIE

Most spaghetti pies use pasta as a crust. This luscious favorite is reversed so the spaghetti tops the meat. Don't forget to sprinkle with Parmesan cheese.

Prep: 20 minutes
Bake: 50 minutes
Stand: 15 minutes
Oven: 350°F
Makes: 6 servings

1   **5-ounce can (⅔ cup) evaporated milk**

½   **cup fine dry bread crumbs**

⅓   **cup chopped onion (1 small)**

1   **teaspoon salt**

1   **teaspoon dried Italian seasoning, crushed**

¼   **teaspoon black pepper**

1   **pound lean ground beef**

4   **ounces dried spaghetti**

1   **tablespoon butter**

¼   **cup grated Parmesan cheese**

1   **beaten egg**

1   **8-ounce can pizza sauce**

1   **cup shredded mozzarella cheese (4 ounces)**

1 In a large bowl combine evaporated milk, bread crumbs, onion, salt, Italian seasoning, and pepper. Add ground beef and mix well. Spread beef mixture evenly over the bottom and up sides of an ungreased 9-inch pie plate. Bake, uncovered, in a 350°F oven about 30 minutes or until meat is brown and an instant-read thermometer inserted into center of meat registers 160°F. Carefully tilt pie plate and drain off fat.

2 Meanwhile, cook spaghetti according to package directions; drain. Return to pan. Add butter and stir until melted. Stir in Parmesan cheese and egg until spaghetti is coated.

3 Spoon half of the pizza sauce over the meat mixture in pie plate. Top with ½ cup of the mozzarella cheese and the spaghetti mixture. Spoon remaining pizza sauce over spaghetti layer; top with remaining ½ cup cheese. Bake, uncovered, about 20 minutes more or until pie is heated through. Let stand for 15 minutes before serving.

Nutrition Facts per serving: 373 cal., 17 g total fat (8 g sat. fat), 110 mg chol., 1,078 mg sodium, 28 g carbo., 26 g pro.

baked penne WITH MEAT SAUCE

Make and freeze this casserole in individual dishes or in one large dish for a crowd.

Prep: 30 minutes
Bake: 75 minutes or 50 minutes
Oven: 350°F
Makes: 6 servings

8 ounces dried penne pasta

1 14.5-ounce can diced tomatoes

½ of a 6-ounce can (⅓ cup) Italian-style tomato paste

⅓ cup dry red wine or tomato juice

⅓ cup water

½ teaspoon sugar

½ teaspoon dried oregano, crushed, or 2 teaspoons snipped fresh oregano

¼ teaspoon salt

¼ teaspoon ground black pepper

1 pound lean ground beef

½ cup chopped onion (1 medium)

¼ cup sliced pitted ripe olives

1 cup shredded reduced-fat mozzarella cheese (4 ounces)

1 Cook pasta according to package directions; drain well.

2 Meanwhile, in a medium bowl stir together undrained tomatoes, tomato paste, wine, water, sugar, dried oregano (if using), salt, and pepper. Set aside.

3 In a large skillet brown ground beef and onion over medium heat. Drain off fat. Stir in tomato mixture. Bring to boiling; reduce heat. Cover and simmer for 10 minutes. Stir in pasta, fresh oregano (if using), and olives.

4 Divide the pasta mixture among six 10- to 12-ounce individual casseroles (or one 3-quart rectangular baking dish.)* Cover with freezer wrap, label, and freeze for up to 1 month.

5 To serve, preheat oven to 350°F. Remove freezer wrap; cover each casserole with foil. Bake in the preheated oven about 70 minutes or until heated through. Sprinkle with mozzarella cheese. Bake, uncovered, about 5 minutes more or until cheese melts. (Or, thaw casseroles overnight in the refrigerator. Remove freezer wrap; cover each casserole with foil. Bake in a 350°F oven about 45 minutes or until heated through. Sprinkle with cheese and bake about 5 minutes more or until cheese melts.)

Nutrition Facts per serving: 342 cal., 10 g total fat (4 g sat. fat), 51 mg chol., 465 mg sodium, 37 g carbo., 22 g pro.

*Note: To serve in a 3-quart baking dish: Cover dish with foil. Bake in the preheated oven about 1½ hours or until heated through, stirring carefully once. Sprinkle with mozzarella cheese. Bake, uncovered, about 5 minutes more or until cheese melts. (Or, thaw baking dish overnight in the refrigerator. Remove freezer wrap; cover baking dish with foil. Bake in a 350°F oven about 55 minutes or until heated through, stirring carefully once. Sprinkle with cheese and bake about 5 minutes more or until cheese melts.)

beef-corn CASSEROLE

Serve this hearty dish with something light, such as crisp, fresh apples or pears.

Prep: 30 minutes
Bake: 20 minutes
Oven: 350°F
Makes: 6 servings

1   8-ounce package extra-wide
    egg noodles

1   pound lean ground beef or
    ground raw turkey

¾   cup coarsely chopped green
    sweet pepper (1 medium)

½   cup chopped onion
    (1 medium)

1   10-ounce package frozen
    whole kernel corn

1   10.75-ounce can condensed
    golden mushroom soup

1   cup chopped fresh
    mushrooms

1   3-ounce package cream
    cheese, cut up

⅓   cup milk

1   2-ounce jar diced pimientos

❶ Cook noodles according to package directions; drain and rinse.

❷ Preheat oven to 350°F. In a 4-quart Dutch oven cook ground beef until brown. Drain off fat. Add sweet pepper and onion. Cook and stir for 2 minutes. Add corn, soup, mushrooms, cream cheese, milk, and pimientos. Heat and stir until cheese melts. Gently stir in noodles. Spread meat mixture in an ungreased 2-quart rectangular baking dish.

❸ Bake, covered, in the preheated oven for 20 to 25 minutes or until heated through.

Nutrition Facts per serving: 411 cal., 16 g total fat (7 g sat. fat), 102 mg chol., 478 mg sodium, 45 g carbo., 23 g pro.

Make Ahead: Place drained noodles in a resealable plastic bag. Seal; chill in the refrigerator for up to 24 hours. Cook beef, adding sweet pepper, onion, corn, soup, mushrooms, cream cheese, milk, and pimientos as directed. Cool; transfer to a large bowl. Cover; chill for up to 24 hours. To serve, combine soup mixture and noodles; spread in a 2-quart baking dish. Bake, covered, in a preheated 350°F oven for 75 to 80 minutes or until heated through.

mexican beef AND MACARONI CASSEROLE

Prep: 20 minutes
Bake: 30 minutes
Oven: 350°F
Makes: 8 servings

2 **cups dried elbow macaroni (8 ounces)**

1½ **pounds lean ground beef**

2½ **cups bottled picante sauce or salsa**

1 **15-ounce can black beans, rinsed and drained**

2 **teaspoons dried oregano, crushed**

1 **teaspoon ground cumin**

1 **teaspoon chili powder**

¾ **teaspoon garlic powder**

1 **16-ounce carton dairy sour cream**

¾ **cup sliced green onion**

1 **2.25-ounce can sliced ripe olives, drained**

1 **cup shredded Monterey Jack cheese (4 ounces)**

1 Preheat oven to 350°F. In a large Dutch oven cook macaroni according to package directions; drain. Return macaroni to Dutch oven.

2 Meanwhile, in a large skillet cook ground beef until brown; drain off fat. Stir meat into macaroni. Stir in picante sauce, beans, oregano, cumin, chili powder, and garlic powder. Transfer macaroni mixture to a 3-quart casserole. Bake, covered, about 25 minutes or until heated through.

3 In a bowl stir together sour cream, green onion, and olives. Spread sour cream mixture over top of casserole; sprinkle with cheese, Bake, uncovered, about 5 minutes more or until cheese melts.

Nutrition Facts per serving: 500 cal., 27 g total fat (14 g sat. fat), 93 mg chol., 744 mg sodium, 36 g carbo., 31 g pro.

tacos IN PASTA SHELLS

Just six ingredients make up these shells. But more than convenience, the recipe appeals to the entire family.

Prep: 40 minutes
Bake: 30 minutes
Oven: 350°F
Makes: 6 servings

½ **of a 12-ounce package (about 18) dried jumbo shell macaroni**

1¼ **pounds ground beef**

1 **3-ounce package cream cheese, cut up**

1 **teaspoon chili powder**

1 **16-ounce jar salsa**

¾ **cup shredded cheddar cheese (3 ounces)**

   Chopped tomato (optional)

   Sliced pitted ripe olives (optional)

1 Preheat oven to 350°F. Cook shells according to package directions. Drain shells; rinse with cold water. Drain well.

2 Meanwhile, in a large skillet cook ground beef until brown; drain off fat. Stir in cream cheese and chili powder. Remove from heat; cool slightly. Divide beef mixture evenly among the cooked shells.

3 Spread about ½ cup salsa into one 2-quart rectangular baking dish. Arrange filled shells in dish; top with remaining salsa.

4 Bake, covered, in the preheated oven for 15 minutes. Remove from oven and sprinkle with cheddar cheese. Bake, uncovered, about 15 minutes more or until heated through. If desired, sprinkle with tomato and olives.

Nutrition Facts per serving: 416 cal., 22 g total fat (11 g sat. fat), 90 mg chol., 513 mg sodium, 27 g carbo., 27 g pro.

baked beef RAVIOLI

Prep: 20 minutes
Bake: 20 minutes
Oven: 375°F
Makes: 8 to 10 servings

2 9-ounce packages refrigerated cheese-filled ravioli

1½ pounds ground beef

1 large onion, chopped (1 cup)

6 cloves garlic, minced

1 14.5-ounce can diced tomatoes, undrained

1 10.75-ounce can condensed tomato soup

1 teaspoon dried basil, crushed

1 teaspoon dried oregano, crushed

1½ cups shredded mozzarella cheese (6 ounces)

½ cup finely shredded Parmesan cheese (2 ounces)

1 Preheat oven to 375°F. Cook ravioli according to package directions; drain. Return to pan; cover and keep warm.

2 Meanwhile, in a large skillet cook ground beef, onion, and garlic over medium heat until meat is brown and onion is tender. Drain off fat. Stir in tomatoes, soup, basil, and oregano. Gently stir in cooked ravioli.

3 Transfer mixture to an ungreased 3-quart baking dish. Sprinkle with mozzarella cheese and Parmesan cheese. Bake, uncovered, about 20 minutes or until heated through.

Nutrition Facts per serving: 503 cal., 20 g total fat (9 g sat. fat), 113 mg chol., 854 mg sodium, 40 g carbo., 40 g pro.

frankfurter-pasta
CASSEROLE

Prep: 25 minutes
Bake: 35 minutes
Oven: 350°F
Makes: 6 servings

2⅔ **cups dried medium shell macaroni (8 ounces)**

1 **tablespoon butter, margarine, or vegetable oil**

1 **cup chopped onion (1 large)**

1 **clove garlic, minced**

1 **16-ounce package beef frankfurters, halved lengthwise and sliced**

1½ **cups purchased spaghetti sauce**

1 **cup chopped tomato (1 large)**

1 **4-ounce can (drained weight) mushroom stems and pieces, drained**

1 **8-ounce carton dairy sour cream**

1 **cup shredded provolone and/ or mozzarella cheese (4 ounces)**

1 Preheat oven to 350°F. Cook macaroni according to package directions; drain. Set aside.

2 Meanwhile, in a large skillet melt butter over medium heat. Add onion and garlic; cook until nearly tender. Stir in frankfurters and cook until light brown. Stir in spaghetti sauce, tomato, and mushrooms. Bring to boiling. Remove from heat. Stir in sour cream and ½ cup of the cheese. Stir mixture into the drained pasta. Transfer mixture to a 2-quart casserole.

3 Cover and bake about 30 minutes or until hot. Uncover; sprinkle with the remaining ½ cup cheese. Bake about 5 minutes more or until cheese melts.

Nutrition Facts per serving: 600 cal., 38 g total fat (18 g sat. fat), 73 mg chol., 1,411 mg sodium, 46 g carbo., 21 g pro.

sausage and pepper LASAGNA

A great lasagna is a dish that everyone appreciates. This one has it all—creamy cheeses, robust sausages, and a tangy tomato sauce.

Prep: 15 minutes
Cook: 20 minutes
Bake: 350°F for 50 to 55 minutes
Cool: 10 to 15 minutes
Makes: 8 servings

1 tablespoon extra virgin olive oil

1 medium-size green pepper, seeded and diced

1 small onion, diced

2 cloves garlic, sliced

5 links sweet Italian sausage (about 1⅓ pounds total), casings removed

1 can (28-ounces) fire-roasted crushed tomatoes in puree

1 tablespoon balsamic vinegar

2¼ teaspoons dried Italian seasoning

2 teaspoons sugar

1 container (15 ounces) ricotta cheese

1 egg

4 tablespoons grated Parmesan cheese

¼ teaspoon black pepper

12 no-boil lasagna noodles

2 cups shredded mozzarella cheese (8 ounces)

1 Heat oven to 350°F. Coat a 13×9×2-inch baking dish with nonstick cooking spray.

2 Heat 12-inch skillet over medium-high heat. Add oil, green pepper, onion, and garlic. Cook for 5 minutes, stirring constantly. Add sausage; cook about 5 minutes or until no longer pink, breaking apart with a spoon. Add tomatoes, vinegar, 2 teaspoons Italian seasoning, and sugar. Reduce heat to medium; simmer for 10 minutes.

3 In medium-size bowl, stir together ricotta cheese and egg. Stir in 2 tablespoons grated Parmesan cheese, the black pepper, and the remaining ¼ teaspoon Italian seasoning.

4 Begin layering: Place 1 cup of the sausage mixture on bottom of prepared baking dish. Top with 3 noodles (do not overlap). Top with ¾ cup of the ricotta cheese mixture and 1 cup of the mozzarella cheese. Ladle on 1 cup of the sausage mixture, then 3 noodles and another 1 cup sausage mixture. Top with 3 more noodles, then top with remaining ricotta cheese mixture. Spread with 1 cup sausage mixture; top with the final 3 noodles. Top noodles with the remaining sausage mixture, the remaining 1 cup mozzarella cheese and the remaining 2 tablespoons Parmesan cheese.

5 Cover dish with nonstick aluminum foil; bake at 350°F for 30 minutes. Uncover dish; bake for 20 to 25 minutes longer or until top is browned. Cool for 10 to 15 minutes before serving.

Nutrition Facts per serving: 478 cal., 23 g total fat (10 g sat. fat), 94 mg chol., 818 mg sodium, 36 g carbo., 28 g pro.

italian PASTA CASSEROLE

Prep: 25 minutes
Bake: 30 minutes
Oven: 350°F
Makes: 8 servings

1   1.29-pound package mild or hot Italian sausage links, sliced ½-inch thick (such as Johnsonville sausage links)

1   tablespoon olive oil

1   12-ounce pkg. dried medium shell macaroni

½   cup bottled Italian salad dressing

1   10.75-ounce can condensed cream of chicken soup

1   8-ounce carton dairy sour cream

1   8-ounce pkg. shredded Italian blend cheeses

2   tablespoons all-purpose flour

3   garlic cloves, minced

2   medium zucchini and/or yellow summer squash, halved lengthwise and sliced ½-inch thick

1 Preheat oven to 350°F. In large skillet cook sausage in hot oil until no longer pink, stirring frequently. Drain in colander. Meanwhile, cook pasta according to package directions; drain over sausage in colander.

2 In large bowl combine salad dressing, soup, sour cream, 1 cup cheese, flour, and garlic. Stir in squash and pasta/sausage mixture. Pour into 3-quart rectangular baking dish. Cover with foil and bake 25 minutes. Uncover; sprinkle with remaining 1 cup cheese. Bake 5 minutes more or until hot and bubbly.

Nutrition Facts per serving: 658 cal., 43 g total fat (17 g sat. fat), 91 mg chol., 1,281 mg sodium, 41 g carbo., 26 g pro.

baked rotini WITH HAM

This creamy, colorful dish is a real kid-pleaser.

Prep: 25 minutes
Chill: up to 24 hours
Bake: 25 minutes
Oven: 350°F
Stand: 10 minutes
Makes: 4 servings

8 ounces dried tri-colored rotini
   (3 cups)

1 16- to 17-ounce jar Alfredo
   pasta sauce

½ cup milk

½ cup shredded mozzarella
   cheese (2 ounces)

2 ounces cooked ham, chopped
   (½ cup)

1 teaspoon dried Italian
   seasoning, crushed

⅛ teaspoon ground black
   pepper

¼ cup grated Parmesan cheese

1 Cook rotini according to package directions; drain and return to pan. Stir in Alfredo sauce, milk, mozzarella, ham, Italian seasoning, and pepper.

2 Transfer rotini mixture to four 7- to 8-ounce individual au gratin dishes or ramekins or a 1½-quart au gratin dish. Sprinkle with Parmesan cheese. Cover and chill for up to 24 hours.

3 To serve, preheat oven to 350°F. Cover with foil and bake for 25 to 30 minutes for the individual dishes, or about 45 minutes for the casserole dish, or until mixture is heated through. Let stand for 10 minutes. Stir before serving.

Nutrition Facts per serving: 503 cal., 28 g total fat (13 g sat. fat), 121 mg chol., 1084 mg sodium, 51 g carbo., 20 g pro.

tuna-noodle CASSEROLE

Make an old standby new again: Add green beans and mushrooms and breathe new life into everyday tuna-noodle casserole.

Prep: 25 minutes
Bake: 20 minutes
Oven: 375°F
Makes: 6 servings

2 **cups dried medium noodles (4 ounces)**

2 **cups loose-pack frozen cut green beans**

⅓ **cup fine dry bread crumbs**

2 **teaspoons butter, melted**

Nonstick cooking spray

1 **cup sliced fresh mushrooms**

¾ **cup coarsely chopped red sweet pepper**

½ **cup chopped onion (1 medium)**

1 **10¾-ounce can reduced-fat and reduced-sodium condensed cream of mushroom or celery soup**

½ **cup reduced-fat milk**

½ **cup shredded American or process Swiss cheese (2 ounces)**

1 **9.25-ounce can tuna (water pack), drained and flaked**

❶ Cook noodles according to package directions, adding the green beans for the last 3 minutes of cooking. Drain; set aside.

❷ Meanwhile, toss the bread crumbs with melted butter; set aside.

❸ Lightly coat an unheated large nonstick skillet with nonstick cooking spray. Preheat over medium heat. Add mushrooms, sweet pepper, and onion. Cook and stir until vegetables are tender. Add soup, milk, and cheese, stirring until cheese is melted. Stir in cooked noodle-green bean mixture and tuna.

❹ Spoon noodle mixture into a 1½-quart casserole. Sprinkle bread crumb mixture over noodle mixture. Bake, uncovered, in a 375°F oven for 20 to 25 minutes or until heated through and bread crumbs are golden.

Nutrition Facts per serving: 258 cal., 8 g total fat (4 g sat. fat), 52 mg chol., 651 mg sodium, 28 g carbo., 18 g pro.

macaroni AND CHEESE

Rich and creamy, this savory macaroni and cheese is based on a blend of three cheeses rather than just one. Complete the meal with a beautiful, crisp green salad.

Prep: 20 minutes
Bake: 45 minutes
Stand: 10 minutes
Makes: 8 to 10 servings

10 ounces dried elbow macaroni
    (2½ cups)

 1 8-ounce package shredded
    sharp cheddar cheese
    (2 cups)

 1 8-ounce package pasteurized
    prepared cheese product, cut
    up (1 cup)

¼ cup butter, cut into pieces

 3 eggs, slightly beaten

 1 12-ounce can evaporated milk

 1 10.75-ounce can condensed
    cheddar cheese soup

¼ teaspoon seasoned salt

¼ teaspoon ground white
    pepper

① Cook macaroni according to package directions. Meanwhile, let the cheeses and butter stand at room temperature. Drain macaroni; transfer to a very large bowl. Add 1 cup of the shredded cheddar and the cheese product to the hot pasta, stirring until the cheeses start to melt.

② In a medium bowl whisk together eggs, the softened butter, milk, cheese soup, seasoned salt and white pepper. Stir egg mixture into macaroni mixture. Transfer half of the mixture to a 3-quart rectangular baking dish. Sprinkle with ½ cup of the shredded cheddar. Top with remaining macaroni mixture.

③ Bake, covered, in a 325°F oven for 30 minutes. Uncover; sprinkle with the remaining ½ cup shredded cheddar. Return to oven. Bake about 15 minutes more or until cheese is melted and mixture is bubbly and heated through. Let stand 10 minutes before serving.

Nutrition Facts per serving: 514 cal., 29 g total fat (18 g sat. fat), 163 mg chol., 1,023 mg sodium, 37 g carbo., 24 g pro.

greek PASTA CASSEROLE

Cooks from countries bordering the Mediterranean know how to stretch the meat—or leave it out entirely—and still serve fully satisfying, full-flavor meals. This lively Greek-inspired casserole is proof positive!

Prep: 25 minutes
Bake: 20 minutes
Oven: 375°F
Stand: 10 minutes
Makes: 6 servings

12 ounces dried rotini pasta
    (3½ cups)

 1 15-ounce can tomato sauce

 1 10.75-ounce can condensed
    tomato soup

 1 15-ounce can white kidney
    beans (cannellini beans) or
    garbanzo beans (chickpeas),
    rinsed and drained

 8 ounces feta cheese, crumbled
    (2 cups)

 1 cup coarsely chopped pitted
    Greek black olives

 ½ cup seasoned fine dry bread
    crumbs

 2 tablespoons butter or
    margarine, melted

 2 tablespoons finely shredded
    or grated Parmesan cheese

1 Cook pasta according to package directions. Drain. In a very large bowl combine cooked pasta, tomato sauce, and tomato soup; toss to coat. Stir in beans, cheese, and olives.

2 Spoon pasta mixture into a lightly greased 3-quart rectangular baking dish. In a small bowl stir together bread crumbs, melted butter, and Parmesan cheese; sprinkle over pasta mixture.

3 Bake, uncovered, in a 375°F oven for 20 to 25 minutes or until heated through and top is lightly browned. Let stand for 10 minutes before serving.

Nutrition Facts per serving: 553 cal., 19 g total fat (10 g sat. fat), 52 mg chol., 1,890 mg sodium, 74 g carbo., 24 g pro.

black bean LASAGNA

Cheesy and rich-tasting, this vegetarian casserole will please the calorie watchers on your guest list. To spice it up even more, use a chunky chili-tomato sauce.

Prep: 45 minutes
Bake: 40 minutes
Oven: 350°F
Makes: 8 servings

9 **lasagna noodles (8 ounces)**

2 **15-ounce cans black beans, rinsed and drained**

Nonstick cooking spray

½ **cup chopped onion**

½ **cup chopped green sweet pepper**

2 **cloves garlic, minced**

2 **15-ounce cans low-sodium tomato sauce or tomato sauce with seasonings**

¼ **cup snipped fresh cilantro**

1 **12-ounce container low-fat cottage cheese**

1 **8-ounce package reduced-fat cream cheese (Neufchatel)**

¼ **cup light dairy sour cream**

Tomato slices (optional)

Fresh cilantro leaves (optional)

1 Cook noodles according to package directions; drain. Mash 1 can of the beans; set aside.

2 Lightly coat a large skillet with cooking spray; add onion, green sweet pepper, and garlic. Cook and stir over medium heat until tender but not brown. Add mashed beans, unmashed beans, tomato sauce, and snipped cilantro; heat through.

3 In a large bowl combine cottage cheese, cream cheese, and sour cream; set aside. Spray a 13x9x2-inch baking dish or 3-quart rectangular casserole with nonstick coating. Arrange 3 noodles in the dish. Top with one-third of the bean mixture. Spread with one-third of the cheese mixture. Repeat layers twice, ending with bean mixture. Reserve the remaining cheese mixture.

4 Bake, covered, in a 350°F oven for 40 to 45 minutes or until heated through. Dollop with reserved cheese mixture. Let stand for 10 minutes. Garnish with tomato slices and cilantro, if desired.

Nutrition Facts per serving: 340 cal., 8 g total fat (5 g sat. fat), 25 mg chol., 589 mg sodium, 49 g carbo., 21 g pro.

Make Ahead: Refrigerate unbaked casserole, covered, up to 1 day, and bake as directed. Or freeze up to 1 month; thaw frozen casserole in refrigerator overnight, and bake for 40 to 45 minutes or until heated through.

tofu MANICOTTI

Your family will love this meatless version of the ever-favorite casserole.

Prep: 40 minutes
Bake: 30 minutes + 2 minutes
Oven: 350°F
Stand: 10 minutes
Makes: 4 servings

8   dried manicotti shells

Nonstick cooking spray

1   cup chopped fresh
     mushrooms

½   cup chopped green onions

1   teaspoon dried Italian
     seasoning, crushed

1   12- to 16-ounce package
     soft tofu (fresh bean curd),
     drained

1   slightly beaten egg

¼   cup finely shredded Parmesan
     cheese (1 ounce)

1   11-ounce can condensed
     tomato bisque soup

1   14.5-ounce can diced
     tomatoes with basil,
     oregano, and garlic,
     undrained

⅛   teaspoon black pepper

¾   cup shredded Italian blend
     cheese (3 ounces)

1 Cook manicotti shells according to package directions; drain. Rinse in cold water; drain.

2 Coat an unheated medium skillet with nonstick cooking spray. Preheat skillet over medium heat. Add mushrooms and green onions; cook until tender. Stir in Italian seasoning; set aside.

3 In a medium bowl mash tofu. Stir in mushroom mixture, egg, and Parmesan cheese. Stuff each manicotti shell with about ¼ cup of the tofu mixture. Arrange stuffed shells in a single layer in an ungreased 3-quart rectangular baking dish.

4 In a medium bowl stir together tomato bisque soup, undrained tomatoes, and pepper. Pour soup mixture over stuffed manicotti.

5 Bake, uncovered, in a 350°F oven about 30 minutes or until heated through. Sprinkle with Italian cheese. Bake, uncovered, about 2 minutes more or until cheese is melted. Let stand for 10 minutes before serving.

Nutrition Facts per serving: 411 cal., 13 g total fat (6 g sat. fat), 74 mg chol., 1,383 mg sodium, 53 g carbo., 21 g pro.

rigatoni WITH VEGETABLES

A robust baked pasta bursting with eggplant, zucchini, mushrooms, and onions makes up this satisfying meatless main dish.

Prep: 30 minutes
Bake: 50 minutes
Oven: 450°F
Makes: 6 servings

Vegetable cooking spray

2 teaspoons garlic-flavored olive oil

1 eggplant (about 1 pound), peeled and cubed

2 medium zucchini, cubed

1 package (10 ounces) mushrooms, diced

1 medium onion, diced

½ teaspoon salt

¼ teaspoon freshly ground black pepper

2 cups prepared marinara sauce

½ pound dried rigatoni, cooked according to package directions

¼ cup freshly grated Parmesan cheese

1 cup shredded reduced-fat mozzarella cheese

Fresh rosemary sprigs, (optional)

1 Heat oven to 450°F. Lightly coat two jelly-roll pans with vegetable cooking spray. Drizzle oil over eggplant, zucchini, mushrooms, and onion; toss. Arrange vegetables on both pans. Sprinkle with salt and pepper. Roast 30 minutes or until vegetables are tender.

2 Reduce oven temperature to 400°F. Spread ½ cup of the marinara sauce over bottom of 13x9-inch baking dish. Combine pasta, vegetables, 1 cup of the marinara sauce and Parmesan in bowl. Spoon into prepared dish. Spread remaining ½ cup marinara sauce over top and sprinkle with mozzarella cheese. Bake 20 to 25 minutes or until bubbly. Garnish with rosemary.

Nutrition Facts per serving: 380 cal., 11.5 g total fat (3 g sat. fat), 10 mg chol., 1361 mg sodium, 55 g carbo., 17 g pro.

pasta
WITH MEAT

Pasta with Beef and Asparagus, *recipe page 114*

zippy beef, MAC, AND CHEESE

Start to Finish: 30 minutes
Makes: 4 servings

6 ounces dried elbow macaroni or corkscrew macaroni (about 1½ cups)

12 ounces ground beef, ground pork, or uncooked ground turkey

1 15-ounce can tomato sauce

1 14.5-ounce can stewed tomatoes or Mexican-style stewed tomatoes*

4 ounces American or sharp American cheese, cut into small cubes

2 to 3 teaspoons chili powder*

Finely shredded or grated Parmesan cheese

1 In a 3-quart saucepan cook pasta according to package directions; drain and return pasta to saucepan.

2 Meanwhile, in a large skillet cook ground meat over medium-high heat until brown. Drain off fat.

3 Stir ground meat, tomato sauce, undrained tomatoes, American cheese, and chili powder into cooked pasta in saucepan. Cook and stir over medium heat until heated through and cheese melts. Sprinkle individual servings with Parmesan cheese.

Nutrition Facts per serving: 587 cal., 25 g total fat (13 g sat. fat), 93 mg chol., 1,665 mg sodium, 49 g carbo., 40 g pro.

***Note:** If using Mexican-style stewed tomatoes, add only 2 teaspoons chili powder.

spaghetti WITH CINCINNATI-STYLE MARINARA

You'll love Cincinnati's famous version of beefy tomato sauce. Packed with red kidney beans, chili powder, and just a touch of cinnamon. It's always served with spaghetti.

Start to Finish: 20 minutes
Makes: 6 servings

- 2 **teaspoons vegetable oil**
- 1 **cup chopped onions**
- 1 **pound ground beef**
- 2 **tablespoons chili powder**
- ¼ **teaspoon ground cinnamon**
- 1 **jar (14 ounces) marinara sauce**
- 1 **can (19 ounces) red kidney beans, drained and rinsed**
- 1 **pound dried spaghetti, cooked according to package directions and drained**
- 1 **cup shredded cheddar cheese**

1 Heat oil in large skillet over medium-high heat. Add onions and cook for 3 minutes. Add ground beef, chili powder, and cinnamon. Cook, stirring, until meat is browned, about 5 minutes. Stir in marinara sauce and kidney beans; bring to boil.

2 Toss sauce with hot pasta in large serving bowl. Sprinkle with cheddar cheese.

Nutrition Facts per serving: 730 cal., 32 g total fat (13 g sat. fat), 84 mg chol., 727 mg sodium, 77 g carbo., 33 g pro.

one-pot SPAGHETTI

This easy spaghetti recipe lets you cook the pasta right in the tomato sauce, so there's one less pan to wash.

Start to Finish: 40 minutes
Makes: 4 servings

8 ounces ground beef or bulk pork sausage

1 cup sliced fresh mushrooms or one 6-ounce jar sliced mushrooms, drained

½ cup chopped onion (1 medium)

1 clove garlic, minced, or ⅛ teaspoon garlic powder

1 14-ounce can chicken broth or beef broth

1¾ cups water

1 6-ounce can tomato paste

1 teaspoon dried oregano, crushed

½ teaspoon dried basil or marjoram, crushed

¼ teaspoon ground black pepper

6 ounces dried spaghetti, broken

¼ cup grated Parmesan cheese

1 In a large saucepan cook the ground beef, fresh mushrooms (if using), onion, and garlic over medium heat until meat is brown and onion is tender. Drain off fat.

2 Stir in the canned mushrooms (if using), broth, water, tomato paste, oregano, basil, and pepper. Bring to boiling. Add the broken spaghetti, a little at a time, stirring constantly. Return to boiling; reduce heat. Boil gently, uncovered, for 17 to 20 minutes or until spaghetti is tender and sauce is of the desired consistency, stirring frequently. Serve with Parmesan cheese.

Nutrition Facts per serving: 362 cal., 12 g total fat (5 g sat. fat), 39 mg chol., 857 mg sodium, 44 g carbo., 21 g pro.

gnocchi WITH MEAT SAUCE

Prep: 30 minutes
Cook: 10 minutes
Makes: 6 servings

1½ **pounds lean ground beef**

½ **cup chopped cooked smoked ham**

½ **cup chopped onion**

½ **cup chopped celery**

¼ **cup chopped carrot**

2 **cloves garlic, minced**

1 **28-ounce can crushed tomatoes, undrained**

¼ **cup dry white wine (optional)**

1 **teaspoon dried thyme, crushed**

¾ **teaspoon salt**

¼ **teaspoon black pepper**

2 **1-pound packages shelf-stable potato gnocchi**

⅓ **cup finely shredded Parmesan cheese**

Snipped fresh Italian parsley

❶ For meat sauce, in a large skillet cook ground beef, ham, onion, celery, carrot, and garlic until meat is brown; drain off fat. Stir in undrained tomatoes, wine (if desired), thyme, salt, and pepper. Bring to boiling; reduce heat. Simmer, uncovered, for 10 to 15 minutes or to desired consistency.

❷ Meanwhile, cook gnocchi according to package directions; drain and keep warm.

❸ Serve meat sauce over gnocchi; sprinkle with Parmesan cheese and parsley.

Nutrition Facts per serving: 516 cal., 14 g total fat (6 g sat. fat), 80 mg chol., 1,440 mg sodium, 66 g carbo., 32 g pro.

penne WITH MEATBALLS

Tender meatballs simmer in a rich tomato sauce seasoned with pancetta and garlic and served over hot cooked penne pasta. This recipe makes enough for two pasta dinners, and the sauce freezes well.

Prep: 40 minutes
Cook: 1 hour, 10 minutes
Makes: 6 servings

- 1 **tablespoon olive oil**
- 1 **can (28 ounces) whole tomatoes in juice**
- 1½ **ounces pancetta or thick-sliced bacon, finely chopped**
- 1 **tablespoon finely chopped garlic**
- ½ **cup finely chopped onion**
- 1 **can (28 ounces) crushed tomatoes in puree**
- 1 **can (15 ounces) tomato sauce**
- ¼ **cup fresh flat-leaf parsley leaves, coarsely chopped**
- 1 **carrot, halved lengthwise**
- 1 **pound ground beef**
- ½ **pound ground pork**
- 1 **cup fresh bread crumbs (3 slices firm white bread)**
- 1 **large egg, lightly beaten**
- 1 **teaspoon chopped fresh rosemary or ½ teaspoon dried rosemary**
- ½ **teaspoon salt**
- ¼ **teaspoon freshly ground black pepper**
- 1 **pound dried penne rigati, cooked according to package directions**

1 For the tomato sauce, heat oil in large Dutch oven over medium heat. Add onion, pancetta, and garlic; cook 4 minutes until softened. Transfer 3 tablespoons onion mixture to large bowl; set aside.

2 Puree whole tomatoes with juice in blender or food processor until smooth. Transfer to Dutch oven; add crushed tomatoes, tomato sauce, parsley and carrot. Bring to boil. Reduce heat and simmer about 10 to 15 minutes.

3 Meanwhile, for the meatballs, lightly mix beef, pork, bread crumbs, egg, rosemary, salt and pepper in large bowl with reserved 3 tablespoons onion mixture just until blended. Shape into twenty 1½-inch meatballs. Carefully drop meatballs one at a time into simmering sauce. Cover and simmer 45 minutes. Uncover and simmer sauce 10 minutes more; discard carrot. (Makes 6 cups tomato sauce and 20 meatballs.)

4 Toss hot pasta with 1½ cups of the tomato tauce in large serving bowl. Top with 1½ cups more sauce and 10 meatballs. (Reserve remaining tomato sauce and meatballs for another use. Freeze in airtight container up to 1 month.)

Nutrition Facts per serving: 505 cal., 17.5 g total fat (6.5 g sat. fat), 65 mg chol., 396 mg sodium, 64 g carbo., 21 g pro.

pasta WITH BABY SALISBURY STEAKS

Start to Finish: 45 minutes
Makes: 4 servings

Nonstick cooking spray

8 ounces mafalda or tagliatelle pasta

2 slices raisin bread or cinnamon-raisin bread, torn into small pieces

¼ cup milk

1 pound lean ground beef

½ cup finely chopped onion

1 egg, lightly beaten

½ teaspoon dried oregano, crushed

¼ teaspoon salt

2 cups sliced zucchini and/or summer squash

1 tablespoon olive oil

1 26-ounce jar prepared pasta sauce

Finely shredded Parmesan cheese (optional)

1 Preheat broiler. Lightly coat the rack of a broiler pan with nonstick cooking spray; set aside.

2 In a large saucepan cook pasta according to package directions. Drain pasta; set aside. Meanwhile, stir together bread and milk in large bowl; let stand for 5 minutes. Add ground beef, onion, egg, oregano, and salt. Mix well. Place a piece of waxed paper on a large cutting board. Pat meat mixture into a 8x6-inch rectangle on the waxed paper. Invert cutting board onto prepared rack of broiler pan. Discard waxed paper. Broil meat 4 to 5 inches from the heat about 20 minutes, turning once, or until a thermometer inserted through side of meat into center portion registers 160°F or until meat is no longer pink inside. Using a long sharp knife, cut into four 4x3 inch rectangles. Cut each rectangle diagonally forming two triangles.

3 In the pasta pan cook the zucchini or summer squash in hot oil for 2 to 3 minutes or until crisp-tender. Stir in pasta sauce and pasta and heat through.

4 Serve steaks with pasta mixture. Sprinkle each serving with cheese, if desired.

Nutrition Facts per serving: 618 cal., 20 g total fat (7 g sat. fat), 131 mg chol., 1254 mg sodium, 76 g carbo., 37 g pro.

mama's AMAZING ZITI

Prep: 20 minutes
Cook: 25 minutes
Makes: 6 servings

- 1 pound 95%-lean ground beef
- 2 cups shredded carrot
- 2 10.75-ounce cans reduced-fat and reduced-sodium condensed tomato soup
- 2½ cups water
- 8 ounces dried cut ziti pasta (about 2½ cups)
- 2 tablespoons snipped fresh basil or 2 teaspoons dried basil, crushed
- 1 teaspoon onion powder
- 1 teaspoon garlic powder
- 1 cup shredded part-skim mozzarella cheese (4 ounces)
- ¼ cup shredded Parmesan cheese (1 ounce)

1 In a 4-quart Dutch oven cook ground beef and shredded carrot over medium heat until meat is brown. Drain off fat. Stir tomato soup, the water, uncooked ziti, dried basil (if using), onion powder, and garlic powder into meat mixture in Dutch oven.

2 Bring mixture to boiling; reduce heat. Cover and cook about 25 minutes or until ziti is tender, stirring occasionally. Stir in fresh basil (if using) and mozzarella cheese. Sprinkle individual servings with Parmesan cheese.

Nutrition Facts per serving: 420 cal., 11 g total fat (4 g sat. fat), 73 mg chol., 649 mg sodium, 49 g carbo., 32 g pro.

round steak WITH HERBS

Tender steak, noodles, and a wonderfully rich sauce—based on cream of celery soup—team up in this main dish the family will love.

Prep: 20 minutes
Cook: 10 to 12 hours (low) or
　　　　5 to 6 hours (high)
Makes: 6 servings

2　**lb. boneless beef round steak,**
　　cut ¾-inch thick

1　**medium onion, sliced**

1　**10.75-ounce can condensed**
　　cream of celery soup

½　**teaspoon dried oregano,**
　　crushed

¼　**teaspoon dried thyme,**
　　crushed

¼　**teaspoon ground black**
　　pepper

4　**cups hot cooked noodles**

1 Trim fat from round steak. Cut meat into 6 serving-size pieces. Place onion in a 3½- or 4-quart slow cooker; place steak pieces over onion. In medium bowl combine cream of celery soup, oregano, thyme, and pepper; pour over meat.

2 Cover and cook on low-heat setting for 10 to 12 hours or on high-heat setting for 5 to 6 hours.

3 To serve, cut meat into bite-size pieces. Toss meat and sauce with noodles.

Nutrition Facts per serving: 392 cal., 11 g total fat (3 g sat. fat), 113 mg chol., 483 mg sodium, 32 g carbo., 39 g pro.

red pepper AND STEAK FETTUCCINE

Start the flavorful sauce by giving the roasted peppers and salsa a whirl in the food processor. A little sugar and some chicken broth round out the flavors, while sour cream adds a tangy richness.

Start to Finish: 25 minutes
Makes: 3 or 4 servings

- 1 **9-ounce package refrigerated fettuccine or linguine**
- 1 **cup fresh pea pods (4 ounces)**
- 6 **ounces cooked beef, cut into ¼-inch slices**
- ¼ **cup dairy sour cream**
- 1½ **teaspoons all-purpose flour**
- 1 **cup bottled roasted red sweet peppers, drained**
- 2 **tablespoons bottled salsa**
- ½ **teaspoon sugar**
- ½ **cup chicken broth**

1 Cook pasta and pea pods according to pasta package directions; drain. Return pasta mixture to pan; cover and keep warm. Meanwhile, cut meat into bite-size pieces. In a small bowl combine sour cream and flour; set aside.

2 For sauce, in a food processor or blender combine roasted peppers, salsa, and sugar. Cover and process or blend until nearly smooth. Transfer mixture to a small saucepan. Stir in broth.

3 Cook and stir over medium heat until bubbly. Stir in sour cream mixture. Cook and stir for 1 minute more. Stir in meat; heat through. Pour sauce over pasta mixture; toss gently to coat.

Nutrition Facts per serving: 440 cal., 12 g total fat (5 g sat. fat), 111 mg chol., 295 mg sodium, 54 g carbo., 29 g pro.

pasta with beef AND ASPARAGUS

Whenever asparagus and steak get together, the result is both elegant and delicious. This dish may appear complicated, but it comes together in almost no time.

Start to Finish: 30 minutes
Makes: 4 servings

- 8 **ounces boneless beef top sirloin steak**
- 1 **pound fresh asparagus**
- 8 **ounces dried bow tie pasta**
- 1 **8-ounce carton light dairy sour cream**
- 2 **tablespoons all-purpose flour**
- ⅔ **cup water**
- 1 **tablespoon honey**
- ½ **teaspoon salt**
- ¼ **teaspoon black pepper**
- 2 **tablespoons finely chopped shallot**
- 1 **teaspoon cooking oil**
- 2 **teaspoons snipped fresh tarragon**
- **Fresh tarragon sprigs (optional)**

1 If desired, partially freeze steak before slicing. Cut off and discard woody bases from fresh asparagus. If desired, scrape off scales. Bias-slice asparagus into 1-inch pieces; set aside. Cook pasta according to package directions, adding asparagus for the last 3 minutes of cooking. Drain well; keep warm.

2 Meanwhile, trim fat from steak. Thinly slice steak across the grain into bite-size strips. In a medium bowl stir together sour cream and flour. Stir in the water, honey, salt, and pepper. Set aside.

3 In a large nonstick skillet cook and stir the meat and shallot in hot oil over medium-high heat about 5 minutes or until meat is brown. Drain off fat.

4 Stir sour cream mixture into meat mixture in skillet. Cook and stir until thickened and bubbly. Cook and stir for 1 minute more. Stir in drained pasta, asparagus, and snipped tarragon. Heat through. If desired, garnish with tarragon sprigs.

Nutrition Facts per serving: 421 cal., 11 g total fat (4 g sat. fat), 107 mg chol., 373 mg sodium, 54 g carbo., 26 g pro.

lone star steak AND PASTA

Prep: 20 minutes
Cook: 12 minutes
Makes: 6 servings

1 **package (16 ounces) wagon wheel pasta**

1¼ **pounds boneless top sirloin steak, about 1-inch thick**

2 **tablespoons corn oil**

¼ **cup fresh lime juice**

1 **can (about 10 ounces) diced tomatoes and green chiles, undrained**

1 **can (about 16 ounces) black beans, drained and rinsed**

1 **medium-size sweet green pepper, chopped**

1 **cup frozen corn kernels, thawed**

¼ **cup sliced green onion**

½ **cup loosely packed fresh cilantro leaves**

2 **cloves garlic, finely chopped**

½ **teaspoon ground cumin**

1 **teaspoon salt**

Sprigs of fresh cilantro, for garnish (optional)

1 Cook pasta in a large pot of boiling water according to the package directions.

2 Meanwhile, with a knife, trim any fat from the sirloin steak. Cut steak lengthwise in half and then crosswise into ⅛-inch-thick strips.

3 Heat 1 tablespoon of the oil in a large skillet over medium-high heat. Add half of the steak; saute for 1 to 2 minutes or until the meat is lightly browned. Remove the steak to a platter. Repeat with remaining oil and sliced steak.

4 To the same skillet, add the lime juice, canned tomatoes and chiles with liquid, black beans, sweet green pepper, corn kernels, onion, fresh cilantro leaves, garlic, ground cumin, and salt; simmer over medium-low heat for 6 to 8 minutes or until the mixture is heated through and the onion and green pepper are not completely cooked but slightly tender.

5 Add the meat from the platter with any juices that have accumulated on the platter to the skillet; cook, stirring, until heated through, for 1 to 2 minutes.

6 To serve, drain pasta and place on a clean platter. Spoon the meat mixture over the top of the pasta. Garnish with cilantro sprigs if desired.

Nutrition Facts per serving: 558 cal., 12 g total fat (3 g sat. fat), 62 mg chol., 753 mg sodium, 79 g carbo., 37 g pro.

spaghetti WITH ITALIAN SAUSAGE AND SPINACH

Sweet peppers and onions balance the spiciness of this Italian-inspired dish.

Start to Finish: 35 minutes
Makes: 8 servings

1   19- to 20-ounce pkg. uncooked mild or hot Italian sausage links, cut into 1-inch pieces

2   medium yellow or green sweet pepper, cut in bite-sized strips

1   small sweet onion, cut in wedges

1   14- to 16-ounce pkg. dried multigrain, whole wheat, or regular spaghetti

1   teaspoon crushed red pepper

¼   teaspoon salt

½   cup chicken broth

6   cups packaged fresh baby spinach

2   to 3 ounces Asiago cheese, shaved

    Crushed red pepper, optional

1 In 12-inch skillet cook sausages, turning occasionally, for 15 minutes or until no longer pink.

2 Add sweet peppers and onion to sausage in skillet. Cook for 5 minutes, stirring occasionally, until vegetables are tender.

3 Meanwhile, cook spaghetti, with 1 tablespoon salt and 1 teaspoon crushed red pepper added to water, according to package directions. Reserve 1 cup pasta cooking water. Drain pasta; return to pan.

4 Toss sausage mixture and salt with spaghetti in pan. Stir in chicken broth and enough reserved pasta water to thin, Add spinach; toss just until combined and spinach is slightly wilted. Sprinkle servings with Asiago cheese and additional crushed red pepper.

Nutrition Facts per serving: 466 cal., 24 g total fat (9 g sat. fat), 59 mg chol., 745 mg sodium, 41 g carbo., 21 g pro.

broccoli rabe, CHICKPEAS, AND SAUSAGE

Prep: 15 minutes
Cook: 12 minutes
Makes: 6 servings

2 tablespoons olive oil

¾ pounds sweet Italian sausage, skin removed

4 cloves garlic, sliced

1 can (15.5 ounces) chickpeas, drained and rinsed

1 large bunch broccoli rabe or broccoli (about 1 pound), trimmed and cut into 1-inch pieces

¾ teaspoon dried oregano

¾ teaspoon salt

¼ teaspoon black pepper

1 pound gemelli or other short-shape pasta

⅔ cup grated Parmesan cheese

1 Bring a large pot of lightly salted water to boil over high heat.

2 Heat olive oil in a large skillet over medium heat. Crumble in sausage and cook, stirring occasionally, for 5 minutes or until no longer pink. Add garlic during last minute.

3 Stir in chickpeas, broccoli rabe, oregano, salt and pepper. Cover and cook for 7 minutes or until broccoli rabe is tender. Add ¼ cup of the pasta water if mixture becomes too dry.

4 While sauce is cooking, prepare pasta following package directions. Drain, reserving 1 cup of pasta water.

5 Toss pasta with broccoli rabe mixture and ⅓ cup of the cheese. Add some of the reserved pasta water, if desired, to moisten mixture.

6 Serve immediately with remaining cheese on the side.

Nutrition Facts per serving: 540 cal., 18 g total fat (6 g sat. fat), 31 mg chol., 939 mg sodium, 71 g carbo., 25 g pro.

capellini WITH SAUSAGE AND SPINACH

This recipe's step-saving secret? The ingredients create their own sauce as they cook together.

Prep: 15 minutes
Cook: 10 minutes
Makes: 4 to 6 servings

2 teaspoons olive oil

1 pound sweet Italian sausage, cut into ½-inch-thick slices

1 large onion, chopped

2 large garlic cloves, chopped

2 14-ounce cans chicken broth

¼ cup water

8 ounces capellini or vermicelli pasta, broken in half

2 10-ounce bags fresh spinach, coarsely chopped

¼ teaspoon freshly ground pepper

⅓ cup heavy or whipping cream

1 Heat oil in a Dutch oven or stockpot over medium-high heat; add sausage and cook 3 to 4 minutes, turning as it browns. Add onion and garlic and cook 2 to 3 minutes, until lightly browned.

2 Add broth and water to pot; cover and bring to a boil. Add pasta and cook 3 minutes, stirring frequently. Add spinach and pepper and cook, stirring spinach into pasta and sauce, 2 to 3 minutes more, until pasta is al dente and spinach is wilted. Stir in heavy cream. Serve immediately.

Nutrition Facts per serving: 615 cal., 38.5 g total fat (14.5 g sat. fat), 91 mg chol., 1441 mg sodium, 44 g carbo., 24 g pro.

creamy sausage-tomato
ROTINI

Start to Finish: 25 minutes
Makes: 6 servings

12 ounces dried rotini or gemelli

1 pound bulk sweet or hot
   Italian sausage

½ cup chopped onion
   (1 medium)

¼ to ½ teaspoon crushed red
   pepper

3 cloves garlic, minced

1 28-ounce can Italian-style
   stewed tomatoes, undrained

1½ cups half-and-half or light
   cream

3 tablespoons finely snipped
   fresh basil

Finely shredded Romano
   cheese (optional)

1 In a large saucepan cook pasta according to package directions. Meanwhile, for sauce, in a large skillet cook the sausage, onion, red pepper, and garlic over medium heat until sausage is brown. Drain off fat.

2 Stir the undrained tomatoes into the sausage mixture. Bring to boiling; reduce heat. Boil gently, uncovered, for 5 to 7 minutes or until most of the liquid has evaporated. Stir in the half-and-half. Simmer about 4 minutes more or until mixture thickens slightly.

3 Drain pasta; return to saucepan. Add sauce to pasta; toss lightly to coat. Sprinkle with basil. If desired, pass Romano cheese.

Nutrition Facts per serving: 568 cal., 26 g total fat (11 g sat. fat), 73 mg chol., 724 mg sodium, 56 g carbo., 21 g pro.

garlic PORK

The exotic flavors of the Orient—fresh ginger, sesame oil, and hoisin sauce—make this hearty stir-fry as delicious as it is easy. Using broccoli slaw saves precious prep time.

Start to Finish: 20 minutes
Makes: 4 servings

 8 ounces fresh Chinese egg noodles or dried fine egg noodles

12 ounces ground pork

 2 teaspoons bottled minced garlic

 2 teaspoons peanut oil or cooking oil

 1 teaspoon toasted sesame oil

 2 cups cut-up broccoli or packaged shredded broccoli (broccoli slaw)

 1 medium carrot, cut into thin 2-inch-long strips

 1 tablespoon grated fresh ginger

 ¼ teaspoon crushed red pepper

 ¼ cup chicken broth

 ¼ cup hoisin sauce

1 Cook noodles according to package directions. Drain. Meanwhile, preheat a large skillet or wok over medium-high heat. Add ground pork and garlic; cook until meat is brown. Drain off fat. Remove meat from skillet or wok.

2 Add peanut oil and sesame oil to skillet. Add broccoli, carrot, ginger, and crushed red pepper; stir-fry for 2 minutes. Stir in broth and hoisin sauce. Cook and stir until bubbly.

3 Stir noodles into vegetable mixture. Stir in cooked meat; heat through.

Nutrition Facts per serving: 407 cal., 13 g total fat (4 g sat. fat), 94 mg chol., 280 mg sodium, 52 g carbo., 21 g pro.

pork LO MEIN

If you prefer, use lean boneless pork, thinly sliced into bite-size strips, instead of the ground pork.
Boneless loin chops also work well.

Prep: 35 minutes
Makes: 4 servings

12 ounces lean ground pork

2 cups sliced fresh mushrooms

1 cup shredded or biased-sliced carrots

½ cup red and/or green sweet pepper cut into bite-size strips

2 cloves garlic, minced

1 tablespoon cornstarch

1 cup reduced-sodium chicken broth

1 tablespoon reduced-sodium soy sauce

1 teaspoon grated fresh gingerroot

¼ teaspoon crushed red pepper

¼ teaspoon curry powder

4 ounces dried thin spaghetti, broken, or linguine, cooked and drained (2 cups cooked)

1 cup fresh bean sprouts

½ cup sliced green onions
   Sliced green onion (optional)

1 In a large skillet cook pork, mushrooms, carrots, sweet pepper, and garlic until meat is brown and vegetables are tender. Drain off fat.

2 Stir cornstarch into meat mixture. Stir in broth, soy sauce, gingerroot, crushed red pepper, and curry powder. Cook and stir until thickened and bubbly. Cook and stir for 2 minutes more.

3 Stir in cooked pasta, bean sprouts, and the ½ cup green onions; heat through. If desired, garnish with additional green onion.

Nutrition Facts per serving: 269 cal., 7 g total fat (0 g sat. fat), 40 mg chol., 350 mg sodium, 34 g carbo., 17 g pro.

Tip: To cook boneless pork, heat 1 teaspoon cooking oil in the large skillet. Add the meat strips. Stir-fry for 2 to 3 minutes or until no longer pink. Remove meat from skillet. Cook the mushrooms, carrots, sweet pepper, and garlic as directed. Return meat to skillet and continue as directed.

grilled pork WITH CREAMY WAGON WHEELS

Prep: 15 minutes
Cook: 12 minutes
Makes: 8 servings

1½ cups reduced-fat sour cream

⅔ cup reduced-fat mayonnaise

1 tablespoon Dijon mustard

1 tablespoon mild molasses

2 teaspoons cider vinegar

¼ teaspoon salt

¾ pound pork tenderloin, cut in ¾-inch cubes

⅓ cup bottled barbecue sauce

¾ pound wagon wheel pasta

1 cup coarsely chopped sweet green pepper (1 small)

1 cup coarsely chopped sweet orange pepper (1 small)

1 cup coarsely chopped red onion

Fresh spinach leaves or other greens, washed and dried (optional)

1 Whisk together sour cream, mayonnaise, mustard, molasses, vinegar, and salt in medium bowl until well blended. Cover dressing and refrigerate.

2 Toss together pork cubes and barbecue sauce in medium bowl. Coat large 12-inch nonstick stove grill pan or heavy regular skillet with nonstick cooking spray. Heat over medium-high. Add pork; cook, turning, until cooked through and internal temperature registers 160°F on instant-read thermometer, about 6 minutes. Remove to large clean bowl to cool.

3 Cook pasta in large pot of lightly salted boiling water until firm but tender, 12 minutes. Drain; add to pork in bowl. Add peppers, onion, and 1 cup dressing; toss. Cover; chill.

4 To serve, pour remaining dressing over pasta; mix. Spoon pasta over a bed of fresh spinach leaves or other greens, if desired.

Nutrition Facts per serving: 418 cal., 14 g total fat (8 g sat. fat), 56 mg chol., 538 mg sodium, 48 g carbo., 19 g pro.

fettuccine with ham AND
MUSHROOM SAUCE

This creamy and satisfying dish may remind you of a vegetable-studded Fettuccine Alfredo. However, you'll find this sauce lighter, since it's made with evaporated milk and without butter.

Start to Finish: 30 minutes
Makes: 4 servings

- 2 **cups sliced fresh shiitake or button mushrooms**
- 1 **small red or green sweet pepper, cut into thin strips**
- ½ **cup chopped onion**
- 1 **clove garlic, minced**
- 1 **tablespoon cooking oil**
- 1 **12-ounce can (1½ cups) evaporated milk**
- 2 **tablespoons snipped fresh basil or ½ teaspoon dried basil, crushed**
- 4 **teaspoons cornstarch**
- ¼ **teaspoon black pepper**
- 6 **ounces cooked ham, cut into matchstick-size strips**
- 1 **9-ounce package refrigerated spinach fettuccine and/or plain fettuccine**

1 For sauce, in a skillet cook mushrooms, sweet pepper, onion, and garlic in hot oil until tender. In a mixing bowl combine evaporated milk, basil, cornstarch, and black pepper. Stir into vegetable mixture in skillet. Cook and stir over medium heat until bubbly. Cook and stir for 2 minutes more. Stir in ham. Remove from heat.

2 Meanwhile, cook pasta according to package directions. Drain. Serve sauce over pasta. If desired, sprinkle with ¼ cup grated Parmesan cheese.

Nutrition Facts per serving: 475 cal., 15 g total fat (6 g sat. fat), 106 mg chol., 677 mg sodium, 58 g carbo., 27 g pro.

triple-smoked PASTA

Smoked Gouda, smoked ham, and chipotle peppers—which are smoked jalapeños—add up to the trio of smoke-enhanced ingredients here.

Prep: 15 minutes
Cook: 15 minutes
Stand: 5 minutes
Makes: 8 servings

3 **cups broccoli flowerets**

1 **pound penne pasta**

1 **tablespoon unsalted butter**

1 **tablespoon all-purpose flour**

1 **cup heavy cream**

1 **to 2 canned chipotle peppers in adobo sauce, chopped**

½ **teaspoon salt**

¼ **cup grated Parmesan cheese**

½ **pound smoked Gouda cheese (rind removed), shredded**

½ **pound smoked ham, cut into ¼-inch dice**

1 Bring a large pot of lightly salted water to a boil. Add broccoli and cook about 4 minutes or until crisp-tender. Remove with a slotted spoon and set aside.

2 Add pasta to boiling water; cook following package directions. Drain, reserving 1 cup of the cooking water.

3 Meanwhile, in small saucepan melt butter over medium-low heat. Add flour and cook for 1 minute. Whisk in cream and bring to a simmer. Add chipotle peppers and salt; cook for 1 minute. Remove saucepan from heat; stir in Parmesan cheese.

4 In large bowl combine pasta, broccoli, Gouda, ham, and cream sauce. Stir in ½ cup of the pasta cooking liquid. Cover and let stand for 5 minutes. Add more of the pasta cooking liquid if needed to attain creamy consistency.

Nutrition Facts per serving: 489 cal., 24 g total fat (14 g sat. fat), 95 mg chol., 793 mg sodium, 47 g carbo., 22 g pro.

greek lamb WITH SPINACH AND ORZO

Prep: 25 minutes
Cook: 8 to 10 hours (low) or
    4 to 5 hours (high)
Makes: 8 servings

1 **tablespoon dried oregano,
    crushed**

1 **tablespoon finely shredded
    lemon peel**

4 **cloves garlic, minced**

½ **teaspoon salt**

3 **pounds lamb stew meat**

¼ **cup lemon juice**

12 **ounces dried orzo**

1 **10-ounce bag prewashed
    fresh spinach, chopped**

1 **cup crumbled feta cheese
    (4 ounces)**

   Lemon wedges

❶ In a small bowl stir together oregano, lemon peel, garlic, and salt. Sprinkle evenly over meat; rub in with your fingers. Place meat in a 3½- or 4-quart slow cooker. Sprinkle meat with lemon juice.

❷ Cover and cook on low-heat setting for 8 to 10 hours or on high-heat setting for 4 to 5 hours.

❸ Meanwhile, prepare orzo according to package directions. Stir cooked orzo into meat mixture in cooker.

❹ Place spinach on a large serving platter. Spoon meat mixture over spinach. Sprinkle with feta cheese. Serve with lemon wedges.

Nutrition Facts per serving: 437 cal., 13 g total fat (5 g sat. fat), 123 mg chol., 445 mg sodium, 35 g carbo., 43 g pro.

pasta with lamb AND FETA CHEESE

Start to Finish: 30 minutes
Makes: 4 servings

12 ounces lean boneless lamb or beef sirloin steak

1 tablespoon olive oil or vegetable oil

1 large onion, cut into wedges

2 cloves garlic, minced

1 6-ounce can tomato paste

½ cup tomato juice

½ cup water

¼ cup cider vinegar or red wine vinegar

1 teaspoon dried oregano, crushed

½ teaspoon ground cumin

¼ teaspoon ground cinnamon

1 medium zucchini, halved lengthwise and sliced (1¼ cups)

2 cups hot cooked orzo (rosamarina) or other pasta

¼ cup crumbled feta cheese (1 ounce)

Chopped walnuts or snipped fresh parsley (optional)

1 Trim fat from meat. Thinly slice meat across the grain into bite-size pieces. In a large skillet heat oil over medium heat. Add lamb; cook and stir for 2 to 3 minutes or to desired doneness. Remove meat from skillet.

2 Add onion and garlic to skillet; cook and stir for 1 minute. Stir in tomato paste, tomato juice, water, vinegar, oregano, cumin, and cinnamon. Add zucchini. Bring to boiling; reduce heat. Simmer, covered, about 5 minutes or until zucchini is tender. Return meat to skillet; heat through. Serve over hot cooked orzo. Sprinkle with feta cheese and, if desired, walnuts.

Nutrition Facts per serving: 349 cal., 15 g total fat (5 g sat. fat), 51 mg chol., 323 mg sodium, 36 g carbo., 19 g pro.

pasta WITH POULTRY

Chicken and Penne with Basil Sauce, *recipe page 134*

chicken and penne WITH BASIL SAUCE

If fresh basil is unavailable, do not substitute dried basil. Use another fresh herb instead, such as thyme, sage, or tarragon. Dried herbs can't compare to the flavor of fresh herbs used here.

Start to Finish: 25 minutes
Makes: 4 servings

1¼ **cups reduced-sodium chicken broth**

4 **teaspoons cornstarch**

⅛ **teaspoon black pepper**

2 **cups packaged dried penne or corkscrew macaroni**

12 **ounces skinless, boneless chicken breast halves**

Nonstick spray coating

1 **medium red sweet pepper, cut into thin strips**

1 **medium yellow or green sweet pepper, cut into thin strips**

3 **cloves garlic, minced**

1 **tablespoon cooking oil**

¼ **cup lightly packed fresh basil leaves, cut into thin shreds**

2 **tablespoons finely shredded Parmesan cheese**

1 Stir together chicken broth, cornstarch, and black pepper. Set aside.

2 Cook pasta according to package directions, omitting any oil and salt. Drain. Cover; keep warm.

3 Meanwhile, rinse chicken; pat dry with paper towels. Cut into 1-inch cubes; set aside. Spray an unheated large skillet with nonstick coating. Preheat over medium heat. Add sweet peppers and garlic. Stir-fry for 2 to 3 minutes or until sweet peppers are crisp-tender. Remove from skillet. Add the oil to skillet; increase heat to medium high. Add the chicken; stir-fry for 3 to 4 minutes or until chicken is no longer pink.

4 Stir broth mixture; add to skillet. Cook and stir until thickened and bubbly. Return sweet peppers to skillet; add the basil shreds. Cook and stir for 2 minutes more. Toss with hot pasta. Sprinkle with Parmesan cheese. If desired, garnish with additional fresh basil.

Nutrition Facts per serving: 330 cal., 8 g total fat (1 g sat. fat), 47 mg chol., 282 mg sodium, 39 g carbo., 24 g pro.

chicken TACO MAC

Prep: 10 minutes
Cook: 21 minutes
Makes: 6 servings

- 1 pound boneless chicken breast halves, cut in half horizontally if large
- 1 box (12 ounces) garden radiatore or rotini pasta (such as Ronzoni)
- 1 sweet red pepper, cored and diced (about 1 cup)
- 1 tablespoon unsalted butter
- 1 tablespoon all-purpose flour
- 1½ teaspoons chili powder
- ½ teaspoon salt
- 1¼ cups milk
- 8 ounces pepper-Jack cheese, shredded (about 2 cups)
- 3 scallions, trimmed and sliced
- 1½ cups crushed lime-flavored tortilla chips

1 Bring a large pot of water just to boiling. Add chicken breast and reduce heat to a gentle simmer. Cook chicken in barely simmering water for 12 minutes. Remove to cutting board; return water to boiling; add a little salt to the water.

2 Add pasta to boiling water and cook as per package directions, 9 minutes. Add pepper during last minute of cooking time. Drain.

3 Meanwhile, melt butter in a medium saucepan over medium heat. Whisk in flour, chili powder, and salt. Add milk in a thin stream, whisking constantly. Bring to a simmer over medium-high heat; simmer 2 minutes. Remove from heat and whisk in shredded cheese.

4 With two forks or your hands, shred chicken into bite-size pieces. In large bowl combine pasta and pepper, chicken, scallions, and cheese sauce. Stir until blended; top with crushed chips and serve.

Nutrition Facts per serving: 557 cal., 22 g total fat (10 g sat. fat), 94 mg chol., 558 mg sodium, 56 g carbo., 35 g pro.

spaghetti WITH GRILLED CORN AND CHICKEN

For a delicious flavor-packed side dish, try this pasta without the chicken.

Prep: 30 minutes
Start to Finish: 50 minutes
Makes: 6 servings

- 4 **boneless, skinless chicken breast halves**
- 6 **ears corn, husked**
- 12 **ounces dry spaghetti**
- 4 **tablespoons unsalted butter, softened**
- 1 **jalepeño, seeded and minced**
- 1 **small clove garlic, minced**
- ¼ **teaspoon ground cumin**
- ½ **teaspoon chili powder**
- ⅛ **teaspoon cayenne**
- 1 **teaspoon kosher salt**
- 1 **tablespoon olive oil**
- 3 **tomatoes, cut into large dice**
- ⅓ **cup chopped cilantro**
- 2 **tablespoons fresh lime juice and lime wedges**

1 Heat grill (or grill pan on a stove). Season chicken with salt and pepper, then grill until cooked through; set aside. Coat corn with a little extra olive oil and grill until just blackened in parts, turning occasionally, 15 to 20 minutes. Transfer to a plate and cover with plastic wrap for 5 minutes. Cut corn from cob and set aside.

2 Cook pasta in lightly salted water. Meanwhile, stir together butter, jalepeño, garlic, cumin, chili powder, cayenne, salt, and olive oil. Drain pasta, then immediately transfer to a large bowl and toss with butter mixture. Gently stir in tomatoes, cilantro, and corn and season with lime juice and salt to taste. Serve with sliced chicken and lime wedges.

Nutrition Facts per serving: 500 cal., 13.5 g total fat (6 g sat. fat), 75 mg chol., 409 mg sodium, 64 g carbo., 33 g pro.

chicken-and-melon-stuffed SHELLS

When the summer heat kills your appetite, fix these plump pasta shells bursting with chicken and melon in a creamy dressing. You won't be able to resist them.

Start to Finish: 25 minutes
Makes: 2 servings

½ **of a medium cantaloupe, halved and seeded**

4 **dried jumbo macaroni shells**

3 **ounces chopped cooked chicken breast**

¼ **cup diced honeydew melon**

2 **tablespoons plain fat-free yogurt**

1 **tablespoon lemon juice**

1½ **teaspoons chopped fresh chives**

½ **teaspoon Dijon-style mustard**

Fresh thyme sprigs (optional)

1 Cut the cantaloupe half into thirds; cover and chill two of the wedges. Peel and dice remaining wedge; set aside.

2 Cook macaroni shells according to package directions. Drain and rinse with cold water. Drain again; set aside.

3 In a small bowl combine diced cantaloupe, chicken, honeydew, yogurt, lemon juice, chives, and mustard. Spoon about ¼ cup of the mixture into each pasta shell. Arrange 2 filled shells and a chilled cantaloupe wedge on each of two serving dishes. If desired, garnish with thyme sprigs.

Nutrition Facts per serving: 176 cal., 2 g total fat (0 g sat. fat), 26 mg chol., 55 mg sodium, 28 g carbo., 14 g pro.

mediterranean CHICKEN AND PASTA

The zesty flavors of the Mediterranean dominate this dish. Artichokes, oregano, kalamata olives, and feta cheese mingle with chicken pieces, garlic, and a splash of white wine.

Start to Finish: 20 minutes
Makes: 4 servings

1 **6-ounce jar marinated artichoke hearts**

1 **tablespoon olive oil**

12 **ounces skinless, boneless chicken breasts, cut into bite-size pieces**

3 **cloves garlic, thinly sliced**

¼ **cup chicken broth**

¼ **cup dry white wine**

1 **teaspoon dried oregano, crushed**

1 **cup roasted red sweet peppers, drained and cut into strips**

¼ **cup pitted kalamata olives**

3 **cups hot cooked campanelle or penne pasta**

¼ **cup crumbled feta cheese (optional)**

1 Drain artichokes, reserving marinade. Cut up any large pieces. Set aside. In a large skillet heat oil over medium-high heat. Add chicken and garlic. Cook and stir until chicken is brown. Add the reserved artichoke marinade, broth, wine, and oregano.

2 Bring to boiling; reduce heat. Simmer, covered, for 10 minutes. Stir in artichokes, roasted peppers, and olives. Heat through.

3 To serve, spoon the chicken mixture over pasta. If desired, sprinkle with feta cheese.

Nutrition Facts per serving: 347 cal., 9 g total fat (1 g sat. fat), 49 mg chol., 323 mg sodium, 38 g carbo., 26 g pro.

fast chicken FETTUCCINE

Refrigerated pasta makes this zucchini and chicken dish even quicker to prepare.

Start to Finish: 20 minutes
Makes: 4 servings

1 **9-ounce package refrigerated fettuccine**

¼ **cup oil-packed dried tomato strips or pieces**

1 **large zucchini or yellow summer squash, halved lengthwise and sliced (about 2 cups)**

8 **ounces chicken breast strips for stir-frying**

½ **cup finely shredded Parmesan, Romano, or Asiago cheese (2 ounces)**

Freshly ground black pepper

1 Use kitchen scissors to cut pasta in half. Cook pasta in lightly salted boiling water according to package directions; drain. Return pasta to hot pan.

2 Meanwhile, drain dried tomato, reserving 2 tablespoons oil from jar; set aside.

3 In a large skillet heat 1 tablespoon reserved oil over medium-high heat. Add zucchini; cook and stir for 2 to 3 minutes or until crisp-tender. Remove from skillet. Add remaining reserved oil to skillet. Add chicken; cook and stir for 2 to 3 minutes or until no longer pink. Add zucchini, chicken, and tomato to cooked pasta; toss gently to combine. Sprinkle individual servings with cheese and season to taste with pepper.

Nutrition Facts per serving: 381 cal., 14 g total fat (1 g sat. fat), 40 mg chol., 334 mg sodium, 40 g carbo., 24 g pro.

thai chicken PASTA

Start to Finish: 25 minutes
Makes: 4 servings

6 ounces dried angel hair pasta

3 cups cooked chicken cut into strips (about 1 pound)

1 14-ounce can unsweetened coconut milk

⅓ cup thinly sliced green onion

⅓ cup packaged shredded carrot (1 small)

2 teaspoons Thai seasoning

½ cup chopped dry-roasted peanuts

1 Cook pasta according to package directions; drain well. Return pasta to pan; keep warm.

2 Meanwhile, in a large skillet combine chicken, coconut milk, green onion, carrot, and Thai seasoning. Cook and gently stir over medium heat until heated through. Pour hot chicken mixture over cooked pasta in pan. Toss gently to coat. Sprinkle servings with peanuts.

Nutrition Facts per serving: 653 cal., 36 g total fat (20 g sat. fat), 93 mg chol., 287 mg sodium, 41 g carbo., 42 g pro.

cilantro chicken PASTA
WITH TOMATOES

Start to Finish: 20 minutes
Makes: 4 servings

8 **ounces dried bow tie or penne pasta**

1 **9-ounce pkg. frozen chopped, cooked chicken breast, thawed**

2 **medium tomatoes, chopped (1½ cups)**

¼ **cup sliced green onions (2)**

⅓ **cup snipped fresh cilantro**

¾ **cup bottled French salad dressing**

1 **tablespoon balsamic vinegar**

2 **slices packaged ready-to-serve cooked bacon, crumbled**

¼ **teaspoon salt**

¼ **teaspoon freshly cracked black pepper**

❶ Cook pasta according to package directions. Drain. In a large bowl combine drained pasta, cooked chicken, tomatoes, green onions, and cilantro.

❷ In a small bowl stir together French dressing, balsamic vinegar, crumbled bacon, salt, and pepper. Pour over pasta mixture; toss to coat. Return to pan and heat through. Serve immediately or cover and chill up to 24 hours before serving.

Nutrition Facts per serving: 558 cal., 24 g total fat (6 g sat. fat), 57 mg chol., 894 mg sodium, 56 g carbo., 29 g pro.

chicken AND NOODLES

Frozen noodles have the thick texture and eggy flavor you remember from Mom's homemade noodles.

Prep: 15 minutes
Cook: 30 minutes
Makes: 8 servings

1 **12-ounce package frozen noodles (about 3 cups)**

3 **cups reduced-sodium chicken broth**

2 **cups sliced carrots (4 medium)**

1 **cup chopped onion (1 large)**

½ **cup sliced celery (1 stalk)**

2 **cups milk**

1 **cup frozen peas**

3 **tablespoons all-purpose flour**

½ **teaspoon salt**

⅛ **teaspoon ground black pepper**

2 **cups chopped cooked chicken**

Coarsely ground black pepper (optional)

1 In 4-quart Dutch oven combine noodles, broth, carrots, onion, and celery. Bring to boiling; reduce heat. Cover and simmer about 20 minutes or until noodles and vegetables are tender. Stir in 1½ cups of the milk and the peas.

2 In a small bowl stir together the remaining ½ cup milk, the flour, salt, and ⅛ teaspoon pepper. Whisk until smooth; stir into noodle mixture along with chopped chicken. Cook and stir until thickened and bubbly. Cook and stir for 1 minute more. If desired, season each serving with coarsely ground pepper.

Nutrition Facts per serving: 269 cal., 5 g total fat (2 g sat. fat), 86 mg chol., 36 g carbo., 19 g pro.

italian chicken AND PASTA

Prep: 15 minutes
Cook: 5 to 6 hours (low) or
     2½ to 3 hours (high)
Makes: 4 servings

1 **9-ounce package frozen Italian-style green beans**

1 **cup fresh mushrooms, quartered**

1 **medium onion, cut into ¼-inch-thick slices**

12 **ounces skinless, boneless chicken thighs, cut into 1-inch pieces**

1 **14.5-ounce can Italian-style stewed tomatoes, undrained**

1 **6-ounce can Italian-style tomato paste**

1 **teaspoon dried Italian seasoning, crushed**

2 **cloves garlic, minced**

6 **ounces spinach or whole wheat fettuccine, cooked according to package directions and drained**

3 **tablespoons finely shredded or grated Parmesan cheese**

1 In a 3½- or 4-quart slow cooker combine green beans, mushrooms, and onion. Place chicken on vegetables.

2 In a small bowl combine undrained tomatoes, tomato paste, Italian seasoning, and garlic. Pour over chicken.

3 Cover and cook on low-heat setting for 5 to 6 hours or on high-heat setting for 2½ to 3 hours. Serve over hot cooked fettuccine. Sprinkle with Parmesan cheese.

Nutrition Facts per serving: 362 cal., 7 g total fat (2 g sat. fat), 111 mg chol., 801 mg sodium, 45 g carbo., 28 g pro.

chicken, broccoli, MAC, AND CHEESE

Start to Finish: 21 minutes
Makes: 4 servings

8 ounces dried rigatoni

2 cups fresh broccoli florets

1 2- to 2¼-pound whole
   roasted chicken

1 5.2-ounce package semisoft
   cheese with garlic and fine
   herbs

¾ to 1 cup milk

¼ cup oil-packed dried
   tomatoes, drained and
   snipped

¼ teaspoon freshly ground
   black pepper

   Milk

   Fresh Italian parsley
   (optional)

1 In large saucepan cook rigatoni according to package directions, adding broccoli florets during the last 3 minutes of cooking time. While pasta is cooking, remove meat from roasted chicken. Coarsely chop chicken. Drain pasta and broccoli; set aside.

2 In the same saucepan combine cheese, the ¾ cup milk, tomatoes, and pepper. Cook and stir until cheese is melted. Add pasta mixture and chicken. Heat through. If necessary, stir in additional milk until desired consistency. Sprinkle with parsley.

Nutrition Facts per serving: 667 cal., 34 g total fat (15 g sat. fat), 163 mg chol., 872 mg sodium, 52 g carbo., 40 g pro.

garlic turkey WITH BROCCOLI AND NOODLES

Chinese egg noodles, ground turkey, broccoli, and carrots are tossed with a bottled hoisin sauce fix-up in this simple stir-fry.

Start to Finish: 30 minutes
Makes: 4 servings

8 ounces fresh Chinese egg noodles or fine egg noodles

12 ounces ground turkey or pork

4 cloves garlic, minced

2 teaspoons peanut oil or cooking oil

1 teaspoon toasted sesame oil

2 cups chopped broccoli

1 medium carrot, cut into thin 2-inch-long strips

1 tablespoon grated gingerroot

¼ teaspoon crushed red pepper

¼ cup chicken broth

¼ cup bottled hoisin sauce

1 Cook noodles according to package directions. Drain. Meanwhile, place a large skillet or wok over medium-high heat. Add ground meat and garlic, and cook until meat is no longer pink. Drain off fat. Remove meat from skillet.

2 Add peanut oil and sesame oil to skillet. Add broccoli, carrot, gingerroot, and red pepper; cook and stir for 2 minutes. Stir in broth and hoisin sauce. Cook and stir until thickened and bubbly.

3 Stir noodles into vegetables. Stir in cooked meat and heat through.

Nutrition Facts per serving: 404 cal., 12 g total fat (3 g sat. fat), 81 mg chol., 436 mg sodium, 51 g carbo., 20 g pro.

orecchiette with kale
AND TURKEY

Ground turkey seasoned with a gutsy blend of garlic, red pepper flakes, fennel seeds, and orange peel is tossed with kale and hot cooked orecchiette pasta.

Prep: 15 minutes
Cook: 17 minutes
Makes: 6 servings

½ **teaspoon fennel seeds**

¼ **teaspoon red pepper flakes**

3 **tablespoons extra-virgin olive oil**

2 **tablespoons chopped garlic**

½ **pound ground turkey**

1 **can (14-ounces) chicken broth**

1 **teaspoon grated orange peel**

¼ **teaspoon salt**

1 **bunch (1 pound) kale, trimmed and chopped**

1 **pound orecchiette, cooked according to package directions**

½ **cup freshly shaved Parmesan cheese***

❶ Heat a 12-inch nonstick skillet over medium-low heat. Add fennel seeds and red pepper and toast 1 to 2 minutes, until fragrant. Add 2 tablespoons of the oil and 1 tablespoon of the garlic; cook over medium heat 2 to 3 minutes more. Be careful not to burn. Transfer oil mixture to medium bowl.

❷ Heat remaining 1 tablespoon oil in same skillet over medium-high heat. Add turkey; cook 3 to 5 minutes or until turkey is cooked through, breaking up meat into small pieces with spoon. Stir in ½ cup of the broth, orange peel, and salt. Bring to boil; boil until liquid evaporates, about 5 minutes. Transfer turkey mixture to bowl with reserved oil mixture; toss to combine.

❸ Add remaining broth, remaining 1 tablespoon garlic, and kale to skillet. Cover and cook until kale is tender, 7 to 8 minutes.

❹ Return turkey mixture to skillet. Cook until heated through. Transfer to large bowl and toss with hot pasta. Divide pasta among six serving plates. Sprinkle with Parmesan cheese.

Nutrition Facts per serving: 455 cal., 12.5 g total fat (3 g sat. fat), 38 mg chol., 591 mg sodium, 63 g carbo., 23 g pro.

*Use a vegetable peeler to shave Parmesan into strips.

turkey piccata WITH FETTUCCINE

The tasty juices and crusty flavor bits left in the pan after cooking jump-start a snappy pan sauce.

Start to Finish: 30 minutes
Makes: 4 servings

- 6 **ounces dried fettuccine or linguine**
- ¼ **cup all-purpose flour**
- ½ **teaspoon lemon-pepper seasoning or black pepper**
- 2 **turkey breast tenderloins (about 1 pound total)**
- 2 **tablespoons olive oil or cooking oil**
- ⅓ **cup dry white wine**
- 2 **tablespoons lemon juice**
- 2 **tablespoons water**
- ½ **teaspoon instant chicken bouillon granules**
- 1 **tablespoon capers, rinsed and drained (optional)**
- 2 **tablespoons snipped fresh parsley**
  Lemon wedges (optional)
  Fresh parsley sprigs (optional)

1 Cook pasta according to package directions; drain. Meanwhile, in a small bowl stir together flour and lemon-pepper seasoning; set aside.

2 Cut each turkey tenderloin in half crosswise to make ½-inch pieces. Dip pieces in flour mixture to coat.

3 In a large skillet cook turkey in hot oil over medium-high heat for 8 to 10 minutes or until light golden and no longer pink (170°F), turning once. Remove turkey from pan; cover and keep warm.

4 For sauce, add wine, lemon juice, the water, and bouillon granules to skillet, scraping up crusty bits from bottom of skillet. If desired, stir in capers. Bring to boiling; reduce heat. Simmer, uncovered, for 2 minutes. Remove from heat; stir in snipped parsley.

5 To serve, divide pasta among four dinner plates. Divide turkey pieces among dinner plates. Spoon sauce over all. If desired, serve with lemon wedges and garnish with parsley sprigs.

Nutrition Facts per serving: 377 cal., 9 g total fat (2 g sat. fat), 68 mg chol., 301 mg sodium, 36 g carbo., 33 g pro.

sage and cream TURKEY FETTUCCINE

Start to Finish: 30 minutes
Makes: 2 servings

- **3 ounces dried spinach and/or plain fettuccine**
- **⅓ cup fat-free or light dairy sour cream**
- **2 teaspoons all-purpose flour**
- **¼ cup reduced-sodium chicken broth**
- **1 teaspoon snipped fresh sage or ½ teaspoon dried sage, crushed**
- **⅛ teaspoon ground black pepper**
- **Nonstick cooking spray**
- **6 ounces turkey breast tenderloin steak, cut into bite-size strips**
- **¼ teaspoon salt**
- **1 cup sliced fresh mushrooms**
- **2 green onions, sliced**
- **1 clove garlic, minced**
- **Fresh sage sprigs (optional)**

1 Cook pasta according to package directions; drain and set aside.

2 Meanwhile, in a small bowl stir together sour cream and flour until smooth. Gradually stir in broth until smooth. Stir in snipped sage and pepper; set aside.

3 Coat an unheated 8-inch skillet with nonstick cooking spray. Preheat over medium-high heat. Sprinkle turkey with salt. Add turkey, mushrooms, green onions, and garlic to hot skillet. Cook and stir about 3 minutes or until turkey is no longer pink.

4 Stir sour cream mixture into turkey mixture in skillet. Cook and stir until thickened and bubbly. Cook and stir for 1 minute more. Serve turkey mixture over hot cooked pasta. If desired, garnish with sage sprigs.

Nutrition Facts per serving: 312 cal., 2 g total fat (0 g sat. fat), 60 mg chol., 478 mg sodium, 43 g carbo., 30 g pro.

turkey and soba noodle STIR-FRY

With a beguiling and nutty flavor, buckwheat noodles (also called soba noodles) from Japan are increasingly popular among western cooks. They're rich in protein and fiber.

Start to Finish: 25 minutes
Makes: 4 servings

6 ounces dried soba (buckwheat) noodles or whole wheat spaghetti

2 teaspoons cooking oil

2 cups sugar snap peas

1 medium red sweet pepper, cut into thin strips

4 green onions, bias-sliced into 1-inch pieces

12 ounces turkey breast tenderloin steaks, cut into bite-size strips

1 teaspoon toasted sesame oil

½ cup bottled plum sauce

¼ teaspoon crushed red pepper

1 Cook soba noodles according to package directions; drain. Return to saucepan; cover and keep warm.

2 Meanwhile, pour cooking oil into a wok or large skillet. (Add more oil as necessary during cooking.) Preheat over medium-high heat. Stir-fry snap peas and sweet pepper strips in hot oil for 2 minutes. Add green onions. Stir-fry for 1 to 2 minutes more or until vegetables are crisp-tender. Remove vegetables from wok.

3 Add turkey and sesame oil to the hot wok. Stir-fry for 3 to 4 minutes or until turkey is tender and no longer pink. Add plum sauce and crushed red pepper. Return cooked vegetables to wok; stir to coat ingredients with sauce. Heat through. Serve immediately over soba noodles.

Nutrition Facts per serving: 331 cal., 6 g total fat (1 g sat. fat), 37 mg chol., 384 mg sodium, 48 g carbo., 25 g pro.

turkey LO MEIN

Colorful, fresh, family-friendly—and fast! Yes, it can be done, thanks to the combined convenience of frozen mixed pepper strips, presliced mushrooms, and stir-fry sauce.

Prep: 10 minutes
Cook: 12 minutes
Makes: 6 servings

- 2 **tablespoons vegetable oil**
- 2 **pounds turkey cutlets, cut into thin strips**
- 1 **package (8 ounces) sliced mixed mushrooms**
- 2 **cups frozen mixed-pepper strips (from a 1-pound package)**
- ⅔ **cup stir-fry sauce***
- 1 **pound linguine, cooked following package directions**

1 Heat a large nonstick wok or large skillet over high heat. Add 1 tablespoon oil. In two batches, stir-fry turkey strips about 3 minutes or until lightly browned. Transfer to a plate and set aside.

2 Wipe out wok or skillet and heat remaining 1 tablespoon oil; add mushrooms and stir-fry for 4 minutes. Add pepper strips and stir-fry for 2 minutes longer. Add turkey and stir-fry sauce and heat through.

3 Place cooked pasta on large platter; spoon turkey mixture on top.

Nutrition Facts per serving: 467 cal., 7 g total fat (1 g sat. fat), 109 mg chol., 1,149 mg sodium, 51 g carbo., 50 g pro.

*Tip: You'll like the way a bottled stir-fry sauce lends zest to this dish. Also try experimenting with the wide range of brands out there to spark your favorite stir-fry or as a marinade.

turkey FLORENTINE

Prep: 15 minutes
Cook: 18 minutes
Makes: 4 servings

4   **turkey breast cutlets (about 1 pound total), cut into 1-inch pieces**
⅛   **teaspoon plus ¼ teaspoon salt**
1   **large onion, chopped**
½   **pound mushrooms, sliced**
2   **tablespoons all-purpose flour**
1   **cup fat-free half-and-half**
¼   **teaspoon ground nutmeg**
¼   **teaspoon hot red pepper sauce**
1   **bag (6 ounces) fresh baby spinach**
2   **tablespoons grainy mustard**
½   **cup shredded reduced-fat Swiss cheese (such as Alpine Lace)**
2   **cups cooked egg noodles**

❶ Coat a large nonstick skillet with nonstick spray. Add turkey pieces, season with the ⅛ teaspoon salt and cook over medium-high heat for 5 minutes, turning halfway through cooking. Remove to a plate and reserve.

❷ Coat skillet with more spray; add onion. Cook on medium-low for 5 minutes, stirring occasionally; add 2 tablespoons of water to prevent sticking if needed. Add mushrooms; cook for 5 more minutes, stirring occasionally. Sprinkle flour over top and stir. Cook for 1 minute.

❸ Stir in half-and-half, nutmeg, hot pepper sauce, and ¼ teaspoon salt. Bring to a boil. Lower heat and simmer 1 minute. Gradually stir in the spinach and cook until wilted. Add turkey and mustard and heat through. Stir in the Swiss cheese until just melted. Serve immediately with cooked noodles.

Nutrition Facts per serving: 397 cal., 6 g total fat (3 g sat. fat), 119 mg chol., 517 mg sodium, 39 g carbo., 43 g pro.

turkey and pasta WITH
PEANUT SAUCE

Start to Finish: 30 minutes
Makes: 4 servings

- 6 **ounces dried fettuccine or linguine**
- 2 **cups fresh pea pods, tips trimmed, or one 6-ounce package frozen pea pods**
- 1 **cup cooked turkey or chicken strips (about 5 ounces)**
- 1 **cup coarsely chopped fresh pineapple or one 8-ounce can pineapple chunks, drained**
- ¼ **cup reduced-sodium chicken broth**
- 2 **tablespoons creamy peanut butter**
- 1 **tablespoon reduced-sodium soy sauce**
- 1 **tablespoon lime juice or lemon juice**
- ¼ **teaspoon crushed red pepper**
- 1 **clove garlic, minced**

❶ Cook pasta according to package directions. Meanwhile, halve the fresh pea pods diagonally. In a large colander combine pea pods and turkey. Pour hot cooking liquid from pasta over pea pods and turkey in colander; drain well. Return pasta, pea pods, and turkey to the hot pan. Add pineapple.

❷ Meanwhile, for sauce, in a small saucepan stir chicken broth into peanut butter. Heat, stirring with a wire whisk, until peanut butter melts. Whisk in soy sauce, lime juice, crushed red pepper, and garlic; heat through.

❸ Add sauce to the pasta mixture. Gently stir to coat pasta with sauce.

Nutrition Facts per serving: 317 cal., 7 g total fat (2 g sat. fat), 30 mg chol., 254 mg sodium, 44 g carbo., 21 g pro.

spicy turkey PASTA SAUCE

Use your family's favorite pasta sauce for this quick and easy dish.

Start to Finish: 25 minutes
Makes: 4 servings

1   **9-ounce package refrigerated fettuccine or linguine**

8   **ounces uncooked turkey Italian sausage (remove casings, if present)**

1   **cup cut-up pattypan squash or yellow summer squash**

1   **small red sweet pepper, cut into thin strips**

¼   **cup chopped red onion**

1   **14-ounce jar pasta sauce**

2   **tablespoons shredded Parmesan cheese (optional)**

1 Cook pasta according to package directions; drain.

2 Meanwhile, in a large skillet cook the sausage, squash, sweet pepper, and onion over medium heat until sausage is brown; drain off fat. Stir in the pasta sauce; heat through.

3 Serve sausage mixture over pasta. If desired, sprinkle with Parmesan cheese.

Nutrition Facts per serving: 350 cal., 10 g total fat (3 g sat. fat), 115 mg chol., 866 mg sodium, 49 g carbo., 20 g pro.

torino turkey sausage
AND PENNE

Prep: 10 minutes
Cook: 15 minutes
Makes: 6 servings

12 ounces whole wheat penne
    pasta

1 large head escarole

2 tablespoons olive oil

1 small onion, chopped

1 package (20 ounces) hot
    Italian turkey sausage

½ teaspoon garlic salt

½ teaspoon black pepper

1 can small white beans,
    drained and rinsed

    Parmesan cheese (optional)

1 Heat a large pot of salted water to boiling. Add pasta and cook 12 minutes. Clean, trim, and chop escarole.

2 While pasta cooks, heat olive oil in a large skillet over medium heat. Add onion and cook 3 minutes, stirring occasionally. Remove sausage from its casing and crumble into pan. Cook 5 minutes, breaking apart with a spoon.

3 Drain pasta, reserving 1 cup pasta water. Keep warm. Increase heat under skillet to medium-high. Add escarole, garlic salt and pepper. Cook 3 minutes, until greens are wilted. Add beans and ½ cup of the pasta water (if necessary). Add drained pasta to the pan and toss to combine. Garnish with Parmesan cheese, if desired.

Nutrition Facts per serving: 431 cal., 12 g total fat (2 g sat. fat), 66 mg chol., 936 mg sodium, 58 g carbo., 31 g pro.

one-pot TURKEY SPAGHETTI

Start to Finish: 25 minutes
Makes: 4 servings

2 cups water

1¾ cups purchased pasta sauce

4 ounces spaghetti, broken up (about 1 cup)

1 pound fully cooked smoked link turkey sausage or frankfurters, halved lengthwise and sliced into bite-size pieces

1 medium zucchini, halved lengthwise and sliced

3 tablespoons grated Parmesan cheese

1 In a large saucepan stir together water and pasta sauce. Bring to boiling. Add broken spaghetti and cook, covered, for 10 minutes.

2 Add turkey and zucchini to pan. Return to boiling. Reduce heat. Cover and simmer about 5 minutes or until spaghetti is just tender and mixture is heated through.

3 Sprinkle Parmesan cheese over each serving.

Nutrition Facts per serving: 352 cal., 12 g total fat (3 g sat. fat), 79 mg chol., 1,585 mg sodium, 38 g carbo., 25 g pro.

pasta
WITH SEAFOOD

Stir-Fry Shrimp and Pasta, *recipe page 168*

stir-fry shrimp AND PASTA

Chinese and Italian cuisines toss together veggies, shrimp, cheese, and pasta. Preparing the vegetables the day before allows plenty of time for marinating.

Prep: 25 minutes
Chill: up to 24 hours
Makes: 4 servings

2 **cups cut up assorted fresh vegetables from salad bar or produce department***

⅓ **cup pitted kalamata olives or ripe olives**

⅓ **cup bottled reduced-calorie Italian salad dressing**

12 **ounces fresh or frozen peeled, deveined shrimp**

1 **9-ounce package refrigerated fettuccine**

Nonstick cooking spray

½ **cup crumbled goat cheese (chèvre) or feta cheese (2 ounces)**

2 **tablespoons snipped fresh basil (optional)**

1 In a large bowl combine cut up vegetables, olives, and salad dressing; toss gently to coat. Cover and store in the refrigerator 4 to 24 hours.

2 Thaw shrimp, if frozen. Rinse shrimp; pat dry. Cook fettuccine according to package directions. Drain; keep warm.

3 Meanwhile, lightly coat a large nonstick skillet with cooking spray. Cook and stir the marinated vegetables in the hot skillet over medium-high heat for 3 to 4 minutes or until crisp-tender. Remove vegetables. Add shrimp to skillet; cook and stir for 2 to 3 minutes or until shrimp turn opaque. Return vegetables to skillet; cook and stir until heated through. Serve over pasta and sprinkle with cheese. If desired, sprinkle with snipped basil.

Nutrition Facts per serving: 364 cal., 10 g total fat (3 g sat. fat), 205 mg chol., 485 mg sodium, 41 g carbo., 28 g pro.

*Note: For vegetables, choose traditional vegetables such as broccoli florets, carrots, cauliflower, peas, and zucchini. Or try sugar snap peas, bite-size sticks of jicama, chopped fennel, quartered baby pattypan squash, mushrooms, or cubed sweet peppers.

thai shrimp AND SESAME NOODLES

If shrimp's not your thing, swap it out for strips of skinless chicken breasts.

Prep: 30 minutes
Cook: 10 minutes
Makes: 4 servings

1¾ **pounds fresh or frozen medium shrimp**

½ **cup bottled Italian vinaigrette salad dressing**

2 **tablespoons chunky peanut butter**

1 **tablespoon soy sauce**

1 **tablespoon honey**

1 **teaspoon grated fresh ginger**

½ **teaspoon crushed red pepper**

2 **teaspoons toasted sesame oil**

1 **8-ounce package dried capellini or angel hair pasta**

1 **tablespoon cooking oil**

1 **cup bias-sliced carrots (2 medium)**

6 **green onions, cut into 1-inch pieces**

2 **tablespoons snipped fresh cilantro**

¼ **cup chopped peanuts (optional)**

❶ Thaw shrimp, if frozen. Peel and devein shrimp. Rinse shrimp; pat dry with paper towels. Set aside. In a small bowl combine salad dressing, peanut butter, soy sauce, honey, ginger, crushed red pepper, and sesame oil; set aside.

❷ Cook pasta according to package directions; drain.

❸ Pour cooking oil into a wok or large skillet. Preheat over medium-high heat. Stir-fry carrots and green onions about 3 minutes or until crisp-tender. Remove vegetables from wok. Add shrimp, half at a time, to wok. Stir fry for 1 to 2 minutes or until shrimp turn opaque. Add the dressing mixture to the wok. Cook and stir until heated through. Return all of the shrimp and the vegetables to the wok. Cook and stir until heated through. Add cooked pasta; toss to combine.

❹ Transfer mixture to a serving bowl. Sprinkle with cilantro and, if desired, peanuts.

Nutrition Facts per serving: 656 cal., 29 g total fat (3 g sat. fat), 226 mg chol., 634 mg sodium, 56 g carbo., 41 g pro.

spicy jalapeño SHRIMP PASTA

Start to Finish: 30 minutes
Makes: 4 servings

12 ounces fresh or frozen large shrimp in shells

8 ounces dried linguine

2 tablespoons olive oil

1 or 2 fresh jalapeño chile peppers, finely chopped*

2 cloves garlic, minced

½ teaspoon salt

⅛ teaspoon ground black pepper

2 cups chopped tomato and/or cherry tomatoes, halved or quartered

Finely shredded Parmesan cheese (optional)

1 Thaw shrimp, if frozen. Peel and devein shrimp. Rinse shrimp; pat dry with paper towels. Cook linguine according to package directions; drain well. Return to pan. Cover and keep warm.

2 In a large skillet heat oil over medium-high heat. Add jalapeño pepper, garlic, salt, and black pepper; cook and stir for 1 minute. Add shrimp; cook about 3 minutes more or until shrimp are opaque. Stir in tomato; heat through.

3 Toss cooked linguine with shrimp mixture. If desired, sprinkle with Parmesan cheese.

Nutrition Facts per serving: 363 cal., 9 g total fat (1 g sat. fat), 97 mg chol., 396 mg sodium, 48 g carbo., 21 g pro.

***Note:** Because chile peppers contain volatile oils that can burn your skin and eyes, avoid direct contact with them as much as possible. When working with chile peppers, wear plastic or rubber gloves. If your bare hands do touch the peppers, wash your hands and nails well with soap and warm water.

shrimp, chickpea, AND FETA CHEESE NESTS

Start to Finish: 30 minutes
Makes: 8 servings

1   14- to 16-ounce pkg. dried multigrain, whole wheat, or regular spaghetti

2   15- to 16-ounce cans chickpeas (garbanzo beans), rinsed and drained

1   16-ounce bag frozen peeled, cooked shrimp with tails, thawed

3   roma tomatoes, seeded and chopped

4   ounces feta cheese, crumbled (1 cup)

2   tablespoons chopped fresh mint

1   teaspoon finely shredded lemon peel

2   tablespoons lemon juice

1   teaspoon dried oregano, crushed

Lemon Wedges

Green olives (optional)

Olive oil

1 Cook spaghetti with 1 tablespoon salt added to water, according to package directions; add drained chickpeas and shrimp during the last 1 minute of pasta cooking time. Drain.

2 Return pasta mixture to pan. Stir in tomatoes, cheese, mint, lemon peel, lemon juice, oregano, and ¼ teaspoon each salt, and black pepper.

3 Serve with lemon wedges and green olives. Drizzle with olive oil.

Nutrition Facts per serving: 696 cal., 14 g total fat (3 g sat. fat), 123 mg chol., 408 mg sodium, 102 g carbo., 44 g pro.

shrimp scampi OVER
LINGUINE

Start to Finish: 25 minutes
Makes: 4 servings

2 teaspoons cornstarch

1 bottle (8 ounces) clam juice

2 teaspoons olive oil

1 pound medium shrimp,
    peeled and deveined

1 tablespoon minced garlic

¼ to ½ teaspoon red pepper
    flakes

¼ teaspoon salt

¼ cup dry white wine

    Pinch dried thyme

1 pound dried linguine, cooked
    according to package
    directions

¼ teaspoon chopped fresh
    flat-leaf parsley

¼ teaspoon grated lemon peel

1 cup seeded, sliced plum
    tomatoes

1 Stir cornstarch into ¼ cup of the clam juice in cup; set aside. Heat oil in nonstick skillet over medium-high heat until shimmering. Add shrimp, garlic, red pepper, and salt; cook, stirring, until shrimp begin to turn opaque, 2 to 3 minutes. Remove shrimp.

2 Add wine, remaining clam juice, and thyme to skillet; bringing to a boil. Stir in cornstarch mixture and return to boil, stirring; boil 1 minute. Return shrimp to skillet; cook until heated through, 1 minute. Toss with linguine, parsley, and lemon peel in bowl; top with tomatoes.

Nutrition Facts per serving: 570 cal., 6 g total fat (1 g sat. fat), 140 mg chol., 415 mg sodium, 90 g carbo., 34 g pro.

citrus shrimp WITH PENNE

Start to Finish: 30 minutes
Makes: 4 servings

12 ounces fresh or frozen peeled and deveined medium shrimp

8 ounces dried penne or bow tie pasta

1 teaspoon finely shredded orange peel (set aside)

2 oranges

Orange juice

½ cup water

1 tablespoon cornstarch

1 teaspoon instant chicken bouillon granules

1 teaspoon toasted sesame oil

¼ teaspoon salt

⅛ teaspoon ground red pepper

1 red or green sweet pepper, cut into ¾-inch squares (about 1 cup)

1 tablespoon cooking oil

1½ cups fresh pea pods, ends trimmed and halved diagonally, or one 6-ounce package frozen pea pods, thawed and halved diagonally

1 Thaw shrimp, if frozen. Cook pasta according to package directions. Drain; keep warm.

2 Meanwhile, after shredding peel from orange, remove remaining peels. Section the oranges over a bowl to catch the juice; set oranges aside. Add enough orange juice to the juice in the bowl to equal ½ cup. In a small bowl combine orange peel, orange juice, water, cornstarch, bouillon granules, sesame oil, salt, and ground red pepper; set aside.

3 In a large skillet cook sweet pepper in hot oil over medium-high heat for 1 to 2 minutes or until crisp-tender. Remove sweet pepper from skillet. Add shrimp to skillet; cook and stir about 2 minutes or until shrimp turn opaque. Remove shrimp from skillet.

4 Stir orange juice mixture; add to skillet. Cook and stir until thickened and bubbly. Return shrimp and sweet pepper to skillet; stir in pea pods. Cook and stir for 2 minutes more. Gently stir in orange sections. Gently toss shrimp mixture with pasta.

Nutrition Facts per serving: 384 cal., 7 g total fat (1 g sat. fat), 129 mg chol., 492 mg sodium, 53 g carbo., 26 g pro.

pasta with asparagus AND SHRIMP

Start to Finish: 30 minutes
Makes: 4 (about 1¼ cup) servings

12 ounces fresh or frozen medium shrimp in shells

6 ounces dried whole wheat bow tie pasta

12 ounces fresh asparagus, trimmed and cut into 1-inch pieces

1 tablespoon olive oil

4 cloves garlic, minced

2 teaspoons snipped fresh lemon-thyme or thyme, or ½ teaspoon dried thyme, crushed

⅓ cup fat-free half-and-half

1 Thaw shrimp, if frozen. Peel and devein shrimp, leaving tails intact if desired. Rinse shrimp; pat dry with paper towels. Set aside. In a large saucepan cook pasta according to package directions, adding the asparagus for the last 2 minutes of cooking. Drain pasta mixture and return to pan.

2 Meanwhile, in a large skillet heat oil over medium-high heat. Add garlic and dried thyme (if using). Cook and stir for 10 seconds. Add shrimp; cook for 2 to 3 minutes or until shrimp turn opaque, stirring frequently. Stir in half-and-half; reduce heat. Heat through. Remove from heat.

3 Add shrimp mixture and fresh thyme (if using) to the pasta mixture in pan. Toss to coat. Serve warm.

Nutrition Facts per serving: 315 cal., 6 g total fat (1 g sat. fat), 130 mg chol., 157 mg sodium, 38 g carbo., 25 g pro.

garlic-basil SHRIMP

Minimal prep work makes this dish great for busy weeknights. A pinch of crushed red pepper flakes adds just the right tinge of heat. If you like it spicy, serve with additional crushed red pepper.

Prep: 15 minutes
Cook: 6 minutes
Makes: 4 servings

6 **ounces dried whole wheat or plain fettuccini**

2 **tablespoons olive oil**

1¼ **pounds frozen large shrimp (20 to 25 per pound), thawed, peeled, and deveined**

3 **cloves garlic, minced**

⅛ **teaspoon crushed red pepper flakes**

¾ **cup dry white wine**

1½ **cups grape tomatoes, halved**

¼ **cup finely chopped fresh basil**

Salt and freshly ground black pepper

❶ Cook pasta according to package directions; drain and keep warm.

❷ Meanwhile, heat oil in large heavy skillet over medium-high heat until hot but not smoking. Add shrimp; cook 4 minutes, turning once, or until cooked through. With slotted spoon, transfer shrimp to bowl (reserve oil in skillet).

❸ Add garlic and red pepper flakes to reserved oil in skillet. Cook until fragrant, about 30 seconds. Add the wine and cook over high heat 1 to 2 minutes, stirring occasionally. Stir in the tomatoes and basil. Season with salt and pepper. Return shrimp to pan and heat through. Serve with fettuccini.

Nutrition Facts per serving: 420 cal., 10 g total fat (1 g sat. fat), 215 mg chol., 216 mg sodium, 37 g carbo., 35 g pro.

rice noodles WITH SHRIMP

Start to Finish: 35 minutes
Makes: 4 servings

1 **tablespoon purchased or Homemade Green Curry Paste***

2 **tablespoons olive oil**

1 **14-ounce can unsweetened coconut milk**

1 **14-ounce can chicken broth**

¼ **cup lemon juice**

2 **tablespoons fish sauce**

1 **14-ounce pkg. wide rice stick noodles**

1 **pound large shrimp, peeled, deveined, and cut in halves lengthwise**

1 **large red sweet pepper, cut into thin strips**

1 **cup fresh snow pea pods, trimmed**

¼ **cup chopped fresh cilantro leaves**

2 **hard-cooked eggs, quartered**

1 In saucepan cook curry paste in hot oil until fragrant and beginning to stick to pan. Add milk, broth, lemon juice, and fish sauce. Bring to boiling; reduce heat. Simmer, uncovered, 8 to 10 minutes or until reduced to 3½ cups. Cook noodles in boiling salted water 4 to 6 minutes or until tender; drain. Rinse under cold water; drain. Divide noodles among four bowls. Add shrimp, pepper, and snow peas to sauce. Return to boiling; reduce heat. Simmer, uncovered, 1 to 3 minutes or until shrimp are opaque and vegetables are crisp-tender. Stir in cilantro. Spoon over noodles. Top with eggs.

*Homemade Green Curry Paste: In food processor or blender combine 1 large onion, chopped; 2 stalks lemon grass, tender white portion thinly sliced; ¼ cup water; a 2-inch section peeled, chopped fresh ginger; ½ cup cilantro; 3 fresh serrano chile peppers, seeded;** 4 cloves garlic, minced; 2 teaspoons curry powder; 1 teaspoon five-spice powder; and ¾ teaspoon salt. Cover; process or blend until smooth.

Nutrition Facts per serving: 781 cal., 32 g total fat (19 g sat. fat), 236 mg chol., 1,402 mg sodium, 96 g carbo., 24 g pro.

**Note: Because hot chile peppers contain volatile oils that can burn your skin and eyes, avoid direct contact with chiles as much as possible. When working with chile peppers, wear plastic or rubber gloves. If your bare hands touch the peppers, wash your hands well with soap and water.

garlicky red CLAM SAUCE

Prep: 20 minutes
Cook: 50 minutes
Makes: 6 servings

2 **tablespoons olive oil**

1 **large onion, diced**

2 **cloves garlic, sliced**

2 **teaspoons sugar**

1¼ **teaspoons salt**

½ **teaspoon black pepper**

½ **teaspoon dried basil**

½ **teaspoon dried oregano**

1 **can (8 ounces) tomato sauce**

3 **tablespoons tomato paste**

3 **pounds plum tomatoes, cored, seeded and each quartered**

1 **bottle (8 ounces) clam juice**

1 **package (1 pound) spaghetti, fettuccine or linguine**

3 **cans (6.5 ounces each) minced clams, drained, reserving ¼ cup juice**

1 In large saucepan heat oil over medium heat. Add onion; saute until slightly softened, about 5 minutes. Add garlic; saute 2 minutes (do not let garlic brown).

2 Stir sugar, salt, pepper, basil, oregano, tomato sauce, and tomato paste into onion mixture until well blended. Add the plum tomatoes. Stir in clam juice. Simmer, covered, 30 minutes. Then simmer, uncovered, for 10 minutes.

3 Meanwhile, cook pasta in large pot of lightly salted boiling water until al dente, firm yet tender.

4 While the pasta is cooking, puree tomato mixture with hand blender or in a regular blender. Return sauce to saucepan. Stir in clams and reserved ¼ cup clam juice; gently heat through, 2 to 3 minutes.

5 Drain the pasta well; transfer to a serving platter. Measure out 4 cups of the sauce and toss with the pasta.

6 Refrigerate remaining 4 cups sauce, tightly covered, for up to 2 days for another dinner, or freeze for up to 3 months.

Nutrition Facts per serving: 358 cal., 4 g total fat (1 g sat. fat), 5 mg chol., 613 mg sodium, 68 g carbo., 13 g pro.

crab and broccoli ALFREDO

Prep: 15 minutes
Cook: 10 minutes
Makes: 6 servings

1 **pound thin spaghetti**

2 **tablespoons olive oil**

1 **small onion, sliced**

1 **sweet red pepper, sliced**

1 **bunch broccoli, separated into flowerets**

2 **cloves garlic, finely chopped**

2 **cups half-and-half**

½ **cup (1 stick) butter**

1 **cup grated Parmesan cheese**

1 **teaspoon salt**

½ **teaspoon liquid hot pepper sauce**

1 **pound crabmeat or imitation crabmeat, coarsely shredded**

Lemon slices, for garnish

❶ Cook spaghetti following package directions.

❷ Meanwhile, heat oil in large skillet over medium-high heat. Add onion and red pepper; cook 3 minutes. Add broccoli and garlic; cook, stirring occasionally, 5 minutes or until tender.

❸ Heat half-and-half and butter in small saucepan until butter is melted. Stir in cheese, salt, and hot pepper sauce.

❹ Add cream mixture and crabmeat to skillet. Heat through over medium heat. Toss with cooked, drained pasta in large bowl. Garnish with lemon.

Nutrition Facts per serving: 750 cal., 37 g total fat (20 g sat. fat), 160 mg chol., 965 mg sodium, 68 g carbo., 36 g pro.

lemony scallops AND SPAGHETTINI

Start to Finish: 25 minutes
Makes: 4 servings

12 ounces fresh or frozen
    scallops

8 ounces spaghettini (thin
   spaghetti)

3 cups small broccoli florets

1 10-ounce container
   refrigerated light Alfredo
   sauce

1 teaspoon finely shredded
   lemon peel

1 Thaw scallops, if frozen. Rinse scallops; drain. Cut any large scallops in half.

2 Cook pasta and broccoli according to pasta cooking directions or until broccoli is just crisp-tender, about 6 minutes. Add scallops; continue cooking for 1 to 2 minutes or until scallops are opaque. Drain well. Return to pan; stir in Alfredo sauce and lemon peel. Heat and stir about 2 minutes or until sauce is slightly thickened.

Nutrition Facts per serving: 119 cal., 5 g total fat (0 g sat. fat), 11 mg chol., 759 mg sodium, 7 g carbo., 14 g pro.

scallop AND BROCCOLI TOSS

Prep: 15 minutes
Cook: 13 minutes
Makes: 4 servings

⅓ **pound whole wheat thin linguine**

1 **head broccoli, cut into florets (about 6 cups)**

½ **cup vegetable broth**

2 **tablespoons reduced-sodium soy sauce**

2 **tablespoons ketchup**

1 **tablespoons sugar**

¼ **teaspoon hot sauce**

1¼ **pounds sea scallops, cut in half horizontally**

1 **can (5 ounces) water chestnuts, drained and quartered**

1 **teaspoon sesame oil**

❶ Cook linguine following package instructions, about 9 minutes. Add broccoli during last 5 minutes of cooking; drain.

❷ In a small bowl whisk together the broth, soy sauce, ketchup, sugar, and hot sauce.

❸ Place the broth mixture in a large skillet and bring to a simmer. Add scallops and water chestnuts and simmer for 4 minutes, turning halfway through, or until cooked through. Remove from heat and stir in sesame oil.

❹ Place cooked pasta and broccoli in the skillet and toss with the scallops. Serve immediately.

Nutrition Facts per serving: 345 cal., 3 g total fat (0 g sat. fat), 47 mg chol., 739 mg sodium, 49 g carbo., 9 g fiber, 33 g pro.

scallops and pasta WITH LEMON-CAPER CREAM SAUCE

Capers and shredded lemon peel add a pleasant zip to this flavorful sauce.

Start to Finish: 35 minutes
Makes: 6 servings

1½ **pounds fresh or frozen sea scallops**

4 **ounces dried multigrain or whole grain penne or rotini pasta**

3 **cups trimmed, coarsely shredded Swiss chard or kale**

1 **medium zucchini, halved lengthwise and bias-sliced crosswise**

Nonstick cooking spray

½ **teaspoon salt**

⅛ **teaspoon ground black pepper**

2 **teaspoons olive oil**

2 **medium leeks, trimmed and thinly sliced**

2 **cloves garlic, minced**

2 **cups fat-free milk**

2 **tablespoons cornstarch**

2 **teaspoons finely shredded lemon peel**

1½ **teaspoons snipped fresh rosemary or thyme or ½ teaspoon dried rosemary or thyme, crushed**

2 **tablespoons capers, drained**

1 Thaw scallops, if frozen. Rinse scallops; pat dry with paper towels and set aside. In a large saucepan cook pasta according to package directions, adding chard and zucchini for the last 4 minutes of cooking time. Drain and keep warm.

2 Meanwhile, lightly coat an unheated large nonstick skillet with nonstick spray. Preheat over medium-high heat. Sprinkle scallops with ¼ teaspoon of the salt and the pepper. Add scallops to hot skillet; cook for 4 to 6 minutes or until scallops are opaque, turning once. Remove scallops from skillet; keep warm.

3 Add oil to hot skillet; reduce heat to medium. Add leeks and garlic; cook for 3 to 5 minutes or until tender, stirring to scrape up any browned bits from bottom of skillet.

4 In a medium bowl whisk together milk and cornstarch until smooth. Add to leek mixture along with lemon peel, rosemary, and the remaining ¼ teaspoon salt. Cook and stir until thickened and bubbly. Cook and stir for 2 minutes more. Add to pasta mixture, tossing to coat.

5 Divide pasta mixture among four serving plates. Top with scallops and capers.

Nutrition Facts per serving: 247 cal., 3 g total fat (0 g sat. fat), 39 mg chol., 525 mg sodium, 28 g carbO., 26 g pro.

salmon WITH BALSAMIC-ROASTED VEGETABLES AND PASTA

Prep: 10 minutes
Roast: 30 minutes
Oven: 425°F
Makes: 4 servings

1 pound fresh or frozen skinless salmon fillets, cut into 4 pieces

2 medium yellow and/or green sweet peppers, cut into 1-inch pieces

8 ounces cherry tomatoes, halved (1½ cups)

2 tablespoons olive oil

1 tablespoon finely chopped fresh rosemary

¼ teaspoon salt

¼ teaspoon freshly ground black pepper

6 ounces dried whole grain pasta (such as linguine, fettucine, or penne)

2 tablespoons dry white wine

2 tablespoons balsamic vinegar

⅓ cup finely chopped fresh basil

❶ Thaw salmon, if frozen. Rinse salmon; pat dry with paper towels. Set aside. Preheat the oven to 425°F. In a 15x10x1-inch baking pan combine sweet pepper pieces and tomatoes. Drizzle with olive oil and sprinkle with half of the rosemary, the salt, and black pepper. Toss to coat. Roast, uncovered, for 20 minutes.

❷ Meanwhile, cook pasta according to package directions. Drain and keep warm.

❸ Remove pan from oven. Stir wine and balsamic vinegar into vegetable mixture. Add salmon pieces to pan and turn to coat with wine mixture. Return to oven and roast about 10 minutes more or until salmon flakes easily when tested with a fork.

❹ To serve, divide pasta among four plates. Top pasta with vegetable mixture and sprinkle with basil. Place salmon on vegetables and sprinkle with remaining rosemary.

Nutrition Facts per serving: 468 cal., 20 g total fat (4 g sat. fat), 67 mg chol., 223 mg sodium, 43 g carbo., 30 g pro.

fettuccine AND SALMON

Makes: 4 servings

1   16-ounce fresh or frozen
    skinless salmon fillet, cut
    into 4 portions
    Nonstick spray coating
⅓   cup finely chopped onion
1½ cups skim milk
1½ teaspoons cornstarch
6   ounces reduced-fat cream
    cheese (Neufchâtel), cubed
    and softened
½   cup finely shredded smoked
    Gouda cheese (2 ounces)
1   tablespoon snipped chives
¼   to ½ teaspoon coarsely
    ground pepper
½   of a 9-ounce package
    refrigerated linguine and
    ½ of a 9-ounce package
    refrigerated spinach
    fettuccine or one 9-ounce
    package refrigerated
    linguine or spinach
    fettuccine
    Chives with blossoms
    (optional)

1 Thaw fish, if frozen. In a large skillet bring 2 cups water to boiling. Measure thickness of fish. Add fish; return to boiling. Reduce heat; cover and simmer until fish flakes easily with a fork, allowing 4 to 6 minutes per ½-inch thickness. Drain; keep warm.

2 Meanwhile, spray a medium saucepan with nonstick coating. Add onion and cook until tender. Stir together the milk and cornstarch. Add to saucepan. Cook and stir until slightly thickened and bubbly. Cook and stir 2 minutes more. Add cream cheese and Gouda cheese. Cook and stir until melted. Stir in snipped chives and coarsely ground pepper.

3 Meanwhile, cook pasta according to package directions; drain. Divide hot pasta among four dinner plates; place salmon atop pasta. Spoon sauce over salmon. If desired, garnish with chives with blossoms.

Nutrition Facts per serving: 566 cal., 26 g total fat (13 g sat. fat), 131 mg chol., 579 mg sodium, 43 g carbo., 40 g pro.

salmon WITH CAPPELLINI

Prep: 15 minutes
Cook: 6 minutes
Broil: 10 minutes
Makes: 6 servings

¾ **cup vegetable broth**

¼ **cup teriyaki sauce**

¼ **cup rice vinegar**

¼ **cup finely chopped candied ginger**

2 **cloves garlic, finely chopped**

3 **scallions, sliced**

2 **tablespoons sugar**

1 **lime**

1½ **pounds salmon fillet with skin (about 1½ inches thick)**

1 **tablespoon cornstarch**

½ **pound cappellini**

½ **pound snow peas, strings removed**

1 **bag (6 ounces) baby spinach**

1 In small bowl whisk together broth, teriyaki, vinegar, ginger, garlic, scallions, sugar, lime rind and juice. Pour into plastic food-storage bag or glass dish. Make several lengthwise cuts into flesh side of salmon, cutting to skin but not through. Place in bag or flesh side down in dish. Seal bag; turn to coat. Marinate 15 minutes.

2 Bring large pot of lightly salted water to boiling. Cover broiler-pan rack with foil. Place in oven 3 inches from heat. Heat broiler.

3 Carefully remove salmon from marinade and place, skin side down, on foil. Reserve marinade.

4 Broil salmon 10 minutes or until fish flakes when tested with a fork.

5 Transfer marinade to small saucepan; stir in cornstarch. Bring to boiling over medium-high heat, about 5 minutes; boil 2 minutes to thicken.

6 Meanwhile, add cappellini to boiling salted water; cook 2 minutes. Add snow peas; cook 2 minutes. Place baby spinach in large colander; drain pasta into colander over spinach, wilting spinach. Transfer cappellini mixture to serving bowl.

7 Remove salmon from broiler. Using fork, remove salmon from skin in pieces. Add salmon to pasta in bowl. Pour marinade over top; toss.

Nutrition Facts per : 263 cal., 1 g total fat (0 g sat. fat), 4 mg chol., 622 mg sodium, 51 g carbo., 13 g pro.

salmon WITH FRESH TOMATO AND OLIVE SAUCE

Salmon receives a Mediterranean-style treatment with tomatoes, garlic, black olives, and a touch of olive oil.

Start to Finish: 40 minutes
Makes: 4 servings

4   fresh or frozen salmon fillets, about 1-inch thick

¼   teaspoon salt

¼   teaspoon pepper

4   large ripe tomatoes, peeled, seeded, and chopped*

¼   cup halved, pitted kalamata olives

1   tablespoon olive oil

3   cloves garlic, minced

2   cups hot cooked tiny bow tie pasta, orzo, or couscous

2   tablespoons shredded fresh basil

1 Thaw salmon, if frozen. Rinse fish and pat dry with paper towels. Sprinkle fish with salt and pepper; set aside.

2 In a large skillet combine tomatoes, olives, olive oil, and garlic. Bring to boiling; add salmon fillets. Cover and simmer for 8 to 12 minutes or until fish flakes easily with a fork. Remove fish from skillet; cover and keep warm.

3 Return tomato mixture to boiling; reduce heat. Simmer, uncovered, about 5 minutes or until slightly reduced. To serve, divide pasta among four dinner plates. Top each serving with a piece of fish and some sauce. Sprinkle with shredded basil.

Nutrition Facts per serving: 402 cal., 17 g total fat (3 g sat. fat), 87 mg chol., 318 mg sodium, 26 g carbo., 35 g pro.

*Tip: The quickest way to peel tomatoes is to plunge them into boiling water for 30 seconds, then rinse them in cold water. Loosen the skin with the tip of a paring knife and slip off the skin.

italian-style FISH

Start to Finish: 20 minutes
Makes: 6 servings

1½ **pounds fresh or frozen white-fleshed fish fillets, ½ to 1 inch thick**

¼ **teaspoon salt**

⅛ **teaspoon black pepper**

2 **cups sliced fresh mushrooms**

1 **tablespoon cooking oil**

1 **14.5-ounce can Italian-style stewed tomatoes, undrained**

1 **10.75-ounce can condensed tomato bisque soup**

⅛ **teaspoon black pepper**

4½ **cups hot cooked linguine or other pasta**

⅓ **cup finely shredded Parmesan cheese**

① Thaw fish, if frozen. Preheat broiler. Rinse fish; pat dry with paper towels. If necessary, cut fish into 6 serving-size pieces. Measure thickness of fish. Place fish on the greased unheated rack of a broiler pan. Turn any thin portions under to make uniform thickness. Sprinkle with salt and ⅛ teaspoon pepper.

② Broil about 4 inches from the heat just until fish flakes easily when tested with a fork. Allow 4 to 6 minutes per ½-inch thickness of fish. (If fillets are 1 inch thick or more, turn once halfway through broiling.)

③ Meanwhile, for sauce, in a medium saucepan cook mushrooms in hot oil until tender. Stir in undrained tomatoes, tomato bisque soup, and ⅛ teaspoon pepper. Cook and stir over medium heat until mixture is heated through.

④ Spoon pasta onto plates; top with some of the sauce, fish fillets, and remaining sauce. Sprinkle with Parmesan cheese.

Nutrition Facts per 3 ounces fish + ¾ cup pasta + ½ cup sauce: 369 cal., 7 g total fat (2 g sat. fat), 54 mg chol., 724 mg sodium, 45 g carbo., 29 g pro.

tuna AND PASTA ALFREDO

Start to Finish: 25 minutes
Makes: 4 servings

3 cups dried mini lasagna, broken mafalda, or medium noodles

2 cups chopped fresh broccoli

1 medium red sweet pepper, cut into thin strips

1 10-ounce container refrigerated light Alfredo sauce

¾ teaspoon dried dill

2 to 3 tablespoons milk (optional)

1 9.5-ounce can tuna (water pack), drained and broken into chunks

1 In a large saucepan cook pasta according to package directions, adding broccoli and sweet pepper for the last 5 minutes of cooking. Drain well. Return pasta and vegetables to hot pan.

2 Stir Alfredo sauce and dill into pasta mixture. If necessary, stir in enough of the milk to make sauce desired consistency. Gently stir tuna into pasta mixture. Heat through.

Nutrition Facts per serving: 545 cal., 12 g total fat (7 g sat. fat), 47 mg chol., 821 mg sodium, 78 g carbo., 30 g pro.

skillet tuna AND NOODLES

Prep: 20 minutes
Cook: 10 minutes
Makes: 4 servings

2 cups dried rotini pasta
(5½ ounces)

2 tablespoons butter

½ cup soft bread crumbs

1 tablespoon olive oil

½ cup chopped onion

½ cup chopped green sweet
pepper

⅓ cup chopped celery

1 teaspoon dried herbes de
Provence

½ teaspoon salt

1¼ cups half-and-half or light
cream

1 12-ounce can chunk white
tuna (water pack), drained

2 tablespoons dry white wine
(optional)

1 Cook pasta according to package directions; drain.

2 Meanwhile, in a large skillet melt 1 tablespoon of the butter over medium heat; stir in bread crumbs to coat. Cook over medium heat 3 minutes or until lightly browned, stirring occasionally. Remove from skillet and set aside.

3 In the same skillet heat olive oil and remaining butter. Add onion, green pepper, celery, dried herbs, and salt. Cook over medium heat for 4 to 5 minutes or until vegetables are tender, stirring occasionally. Add half-and-half; heat just until bubbly. Reduce heat and simmer, uncovered, about 5 minutes or until slightly thickened, stirring occasionally. Add cooked pasta, tuna, and wine. Heat through. Just before serving, sprinkle toasted bread crumbs over the top.

Nutrition Facts per serving: 451 cal., 21 g total fat (10 g sat. fat), 79 mg chol., 725 mg sodium, 36 g carbo., 28 g pro.

spicy snapper WITH LINGUINE

Fresh chiles heat up this Mediterranean-inspired dish.

Prep: 20 minutes
Start to Finish: 35 minutes
Makes: 4 to 6 servings

- 12 **ounces dry linguine**
- 2 **cloves garlic, minced**
- ¾ **teaspoon kosher salt**
- ½ **teaspoon ground corinader**
- ½ **teaspoon paprika**
- 2 **fillets (about 20 ounces) red snapper or flounder, pin bones removed**
- 3 **tablespoons olive oil, divided**
- 1 **medium bulb fennel, thinly sliced (about 2 cups)**
- ½ **Thai chile or serrano pepper, sliced (about 1 tablespoon)**
- 1 **tablespoon lemon zest**
- 1 **tablespoon lemon juice**
- 1 **tablespoon chopped flat-leaf parsley**
- 1 **tablespoon chopped fennel fronds**

1 Cook pasta in lightly salted water and drain. Combine garlic, ½ teaspoon salt, coriander, and paprika and rub on skinless side of fish.

2 Heat 1 tablespoon oil in a large nonstick skillet over medium-high heat. Add fennel and ¼ teaspoon salt and cook, turning occasionally, until golden and soft, 4 minutes. Transfer to a plate, reduce heat to medium and add 1 tablespoon oil. Place fish, garlic side down, in the skillet and cook 4 to 6 minutes per ½-inch thickness of fish (or until fish flakes easily when tested with a fork), turning once halfway through cooking time.

3 Toss hot pasta with chile, lemon zest, and juice, 1 tablespoon oil, cooked fennel, parsley and fennel fronds. Break up cooked fish and gently stir into pasta. Sprinkle with extra zest.

Nutrition Facts per serving: 455 cal., 11 g total fat (1.5 g sat. fat), 42 mg chol., 392 mg sodium, 55 g carbo., 33 g pro.

meatless
PASTA DISHES

Mushroom and Asparagus Fettuccine,
recipe page 209

easy cheesy PASTA

Do what Italian cooks do: Save a small amount of pasta water to stir into the pasta mixture if it is too thick and dry.

Start to Finish: 20 minutes
Makes: 4 servings

8   ounces dried penne, rotini, or gemelli pasta

2   cups frozen cauliflower, broccoli, and carrots

1   10-ounce container refrigerated light Alfredo pasta sauce

¼   cup milk

1   cup shredded cheddar cheese (4 ounces)

½   cup finely shredded Parmesan cheese (2 ounces)

¼   cup chopped walnuts, toasted

1 In a 4-quart Dutch oven cook pasta according to package directions, adding frozen vegetables during the last 4 minutes of cooking; drain. Return pasta mixture to Dutch oven.

2 Meanwhile, in a medium saucepan combine pasta sauce and milk. Cook and stir over medium heat just until bubbly. Reduce heat to low. Gradually add cheddar cheese and Parmesan cheese, stirring until cheeses are melted.

3 Add cheese mixture to pasta mixture; toss gently to coat. Heat through. Sprinkle each serving with walnuts.

Nutrition Facts per serving: 586 cal., 28 g total fat (15 g sat. fat), 70 mg chol., 1,054 mg sodium, 57 g carbo., 26 g pro.

pasta with greens AND ROMANO CHEESE

Here's a way to slip some nutritious greens into your family's diet with this combination of spinach and escarole tossed with curly pasta and sharp Romano cheese.

Start to Finish: 25 minutes
Makes: 6 main-dish servings

- 1 **pound dried fusilli**
- 2 **tablespoons organic olive oil**
- 4 **cups chopped onions**
- 1 **bunch spinach, tough stems removed, or 1 package (10 ounces) fresh spinach, washed and coarsely chopped**
- 1 **large bunch (14 ounces) escarole, washed and coarsely chopped**
- ½ **teaspoon freshly ground black pepper**
- ¼ **teaspoon salt**
- 2 **cups freshly shredded Romano cheese**

❶ Cook pasta according to package directions. Drain pasta, reserving ⅓ cup cooking water. Return drained pasta and reserved water to pot; keep warm.

❷ Meanwhile, heat oil in a Dutch oven over medium-high heat. Add onions and cook until golden, stirring occasionally, about 10 minutes. Add spinach, escarole, pepper, and salt. Stir briefly. Reduce heat to medium-low; cover and cook 5 minutes more or until wilted and tender.

❸ Stir Romano cheese and cooked greens into pasta. Transfer to warm serving bowl; serve immediately.

Nutrition Facts per serving: 489 cal., 13 g total fat (5 g sat. fat), 28 mg chol., 473 mg sodium, 72 g carbo., 21 g pro.

ravioli WITH SPINACH PESTO

Start to Finish: 20 minutes
Makes: 4 servings

1 9-ounce pkg. refrigerated four-cheese ravioli or tortellini

12 ounces baby pattypan squash, halved, or yellow summer squash, halved lengthwise and sliced ½ inch thick

3½ cups fresh baby spinach

½ cup torn fresh basil

¼ cup bottled Caesar Parmesan vinaigrette salad dressing

Shredded Parmesan cheese (optional)

1 Cook ravioli according to package directions, adding squash the last 2 minutes of cooking. Drain.

2 Meanwhile, for pesto, in blender container combine spinach, basil, salad dressing, and 2 tablespoons water. Cover and process until smooth, stopping to scrape down blender as needed.

3 Toss ravioli mixture with pesto. Sprinkle with cheese, if desired.

Nutrition Facts per serving: 218 cal., 6 g total fat (2 g sat. fat), 27 mg chol., 525 mg sodium, 31 g carbo., 11 g pro.

ricotta AND ROASTED RED PEPPER PASTA

Mild ricotta cheese and sharp parmesan cheese create a decadent, creamy backdrop for the roasted peppers and fresh basil in this vibrant pasta dish.

Start to Finish: 25 minutes
Makes: 4 servings

12 ounces dried bow tie pasta
¼   cup butter
½   cup ricotta cheese
¼   cup freshly grated Parmesan cheese
2   cloves garlic, minced
¼   teaspoon crushed red pepper
¼   teaspoon salt
¾   cup coarsely chopped fresh basil
1   7-ounce jar roasted red sweet peppers, drained and chopped (⅔ cup)

❶ Cook pasta according to package directions. Drain and return pasta to pan to keep warm.

❷ Meanwhile, for sauce, in a small saucepan melt butter. Add ricotta cheese, Parmesan cheese, garlic, crushed red pepper, and salt. Cook and stir over medium-low heat just until mixture is heated through. Stir in fresh basil and sweet peppers. Toss sauce with warm pasta until coated. Serve immediately.

Nutrition Facts per serving: 511 cal., 19 g total fat (11 g sat. fat), 52 mg chol., 395 mg sodium, 67 g carbo., 17 g pro.

fettuccine WITH GRILLED SUMMER VEGETABLES

Prep: 25 minutes
Grill: 12 minutes
Makes: 6 servings

- 4 **large garlic cloves, skewered, unpeeled**
- 2 **green bell peppers, quartered**
- 1 **red bell pepper, quartered**
- 1 **eggplant (1.5 pounds), sliced lengthwise ½-inch thick**
- 1 **large red onion, sliced ½-inch thick**
- 2 **large zucchini (1 pound), sliced lengthwise ¼-inch thick**
- 8 **large plum tomatoes, halved lengthwise**
- ¼ **cup olive oil**
- 2 **teaspoons salt**
- ⅓ **cup chopped fresh basil**
- ½ **teaspoon chopped fresh thyme or ¼ teaspoon dried thyme**
- 1 **pound dried fettuccine, cooked according to package directions**
- ½ **teaspoon freshly ground black pepper**

❶ Heat grill.

❷ Brush garlic, bell peppers, eggplant, onion, zucchini, and tomatoes with oil and sprinkle with 1 teaspoon of the salt. Grill vegetables over medium-hot heat,* turning occasionally, until vegetables are tender. (Allow 10 to 20 minutes for garlic, 12 to 15 minutes for bell peppers, 10 to 12 minutes for eggplant, 8 to 12 minutes for onion, and 5 to 10 minutes for zucchini and tomatoes.)

❸ Remove garlic from skin and mash with fork; set aside. Cool and peel bell peppers. Cut bell peppers and remaining grilled vegetables into bite-size pieces. Toss all the vegetables in a large serving bowl with basil, thyme, remaining 1 teaspoon salt, black pepper and mashed garlic. Toss with hot pasta.

Nutrition Facts per serving: 455 cal., 13 g total fat (2 g sat. fat), 72 mg chol., 768 mg sodium, 74 g carbo., 14 g pro.

***Note:** To test for medium-hot heat, you should be able to hold your hand over the coals at the height of the food for 3 seconds before you have to pull away.

mushroom AND ASPARAGUS FETTUCCINE

Mushrooms add rich flavor and meaty texture to this creamy pasta. If you use shiitake mushrooms, be sure to remove the tough stems.

Start to Finish: 25 minutes
Makes: 4 servings

8 ounces dried whole wheat fettuccine or linguine

8 ounces fresh asparagus, trimmed and cut into 1½-inch-long pieces

Nonstick cooking spray

3 cups sliced fresh cremini, shiitake, or button mushrooms

1 medium leek, thinly sliced, or ½ cup chopped onion

3 cloves garlic, minced

⅓ cup vegetable broth

¼ cup evaporated fat-free milk

1 tablespoon finely shredded fresh basil or 1 teaspoon dried basil, crushed

1 tablespoon snipped fresh oregano or 1 teaspoon dried oregano, crushed

¼ teaspoon salt

⅛ teaspoon black pepper

1 cup chopped plum tomatoes

¼ cup pine nuts, toasted

Finely shredded Parmesan cheese (optional)

❶ Cook fettuccine according to package directions, adding asparagus for the last 1 to 2 minutes of the cooking time; drain. Return pasta mixture to saucepan; cover and keep warm.

❷ Meanwhile, coat an unheated large nonstick skillet with nonstick cooking spray. Preheat over medium-high heat. Add mushrooms, leek, and garlic to hot skillet. Cover and cook for 4 to 5 minutes or until tender, stirring occasionally. Stir in vegetable broth, evaporated milk, dried basil (if using), dried oregano (if using), salt, and pepper. Bring to boiling. Boil gently, uncovered, for 4 to 5 minutes or until mixture is slightly thickened. Stir in tomatoes, fresh basil (if using), and fresh oregano (if using); heat through.

❸ Spoon mushroom mixture over pasta mixture; gently toss to coat. Sprinkle with pine nuts and, if desired, Parmesan cheese. Serve immediately.

Nutrition Facts per serving: 319 cal., 8 g total fat (1 g sat. fat), 1 mg chol., 255 mg sodium, 54 g carbo., 15 g pro.

mushroom STROGANOFF

Start to Finish: 30 minutes
Makes: 4 servings

8 ounces dried fettuccine

1 8-ounce carton dairy sour cream

2 tablespoons all-purpose flour

¼ teaspoon salt

¼ teaspoon black pepper

¾ cup vegetable broth

12 ounces assorted fresh mushrooms (such as shiitake, cremini, and/or button mushrooms)

2 medium onions, cut into thin wedges

1 clove garlic, minced

2 tablespoons butter or margarine

2 tablespoons snipped fresh parsley

1 In a large saucepan cook pasta according to package directions.

2 Meanwhile, in a bowl stir together sour cream, flour, salt, and pepper. Gradually stir in the broth; set aside.

3 Remove stems from shiitake mushrooms, if using. Slice mushrooms (you should have about 4½ cups); set aside.

4 In a large skillet cook and stir mushrooms, onions, and garlic in hot butter over medium-high for 4 to 5 minutes or until tender. Add sour cream mixture to skillet. Cook and stir until thickened and bubbly. Cook and stir for 1 minute more.

5 Drain pasta; return to saucepan. Pour the mushroom mixture over cooked pasta; toss gently to coat. Transfer to a serving platter; sprinkle with parsley.

Nutrition Facts per serving: 439 cal., 21 g total fat (12 g sat. fat), 41 mg chol., 419 mg sodium, 54 g carbo., 13 g pro.

broccoli SPAGHETTI

Start to Finish: 25 minutes
Makes: 4 servings

6 **ounces dried spaghetti**

3 **cups broccoli florets**

1 **15- to 19-ounce can cannellini beans (white kidney beans), rinsed and drained**

1 **10-ounce container refrigerated light Alfredo sauce**

3 **cloves garlic, minced**

½ **cup croutons, coarsely crushed**

¼ **teaspoon crushed red pepper**
   Olive oil

1 Cook pasta according to package directions, adding broccoli the last 3 to 4 minutes of cooking; drain, reserving ½ cup of the pasta water. Return pasta mixture to pan; keep warm.

2 Meanwhile, in a blender or food processor combine beans, Alfredo sauce, garlic, and the reserved pasta water; cover and blend or process until nearly smooth. Transfer to a small saucepan; heat through over medium heat, stirring frequently.

3 Spoon sauce onto serving plates. Top with pasta mixture, crushed croutons, crushed red pepper, and a drizzle of olive oil.

Nutrition Facts per serving: 402 cal., 12 g total fat (5 g sat. fat), 18 mg chol., 659 mg sodium, 60 g carbo., 19 g pro.

caramelized onions AND
GARLIC WITH CAVATELLI

Tangy and syrupy Italian balsamic vinegar adds a subtle sophistication to this pasta dish.

Start to Finish: 30 minutes
Makes: 4 servings

10 ounces dried cavatelli or other medium pasta (3½ cups)

2 medium onions, sliced (about 2 cups)

1 tablespoon olive oil

1 teaspoon sugar

1 medium zucchini, halved lengthwise and sliced

4 cloves garlic, minced

2 tablespoons water

1 to 2 tablespoons balsamic vinegar

¼ cup pine nuts or chopped walnuts, toasted

1 tablespoon snipped fresh thyme

1 Cook pasta according to package directions; drain and keep warm.

2 Meanwhile, in a large heavy skillet cook onions, covered, in hot oil over medium-low heat for 13 to 15 minutes or until onions are tender. Uncover; add sugar. Cook and stir over medium-high heat for 4 to 5 minutes more or until onions are golden.

3 Add zucchini and garlic. Cook and stir for 2 minutes. Stir in water and vinegar; cook for 2 to 3 minutes more or until zucchini is crisp-tender.

4 To serve, in a large bowl toss together warm pasta, onion mixture, nuts, and thyme. If desired, season to taste with salt and pepper.

Nutrition Facts per serving: 383 cal., 10 g total fat (1 g sat. fat), 0 mg chol., 5 mg sodium, 63 g carbo., 12 g pro.

chili-sauced PASTA

Start to Finish: 20 minutes
Makes: 3 servings

6 ounces refrigerated linguine
  or spaghetti

1 14½-ounce can low-sodium
  stewed tomatoes, undrained

1 medium green sweet pepper,
  cut into thin strips

2 tablespoons low-sodium
  tomato paste

1 tablespoon chili powder

¼ teaspoon salt

¼ teaspoon garlic powder

¼ teaspoon ground cumin

1 8-ounce can kidney beans,
  rinsed and drained

¼ cup cold water

2 teaspoons cornstarch

1 Cook pasta according to package directions except omit salt; drain. Cover and keep warm.

2 Meanwhile, for sauce, in a medium saucepan combine undrained tomatoes, sweet pepper, tomato paste, chili powder, salt, garlic powder, and cumin. Bring to boiling; reduce heat. Cover and simmer over medium heat for 3 minutes. Stir in kidney beans. Stir together water and cornstarch; add to tomato mixture. Cook and stir until thickened and bubbly. Cook and stir for 2 minutes more. Serve sauce over warm pasta.

Nutrition Facts per serving: 279 cal., 2 g total fat (0 g sat. fat), 0 mg chol., 382 mg sodium, 58 g carbo., 12 g pro.

easy italian MAC

Start to Finish: 30 minutes
Makes: 4 (1½-cup) servings

8   ounces dried bow tie pasta

1   fennel bulb

8   ounces fresh asparagus
    spears

1   tablespoon butter

1   tablespoon olive oil

1   clove garlic, minced

½   cup mascarpone cheese

½   cup shredded mozzarella
    cheese (2 ounces)

¼   cup finely shredded Pecorino
    Romano cheese (1 ounce)

1   cup frozen peas, thawed
    Salt and ground black pepper

1   tablespoon finely chopped
    fresh Italian parsley

1 Cook pasta according to package directions. Drain pasta, reserving ½ cup of the pasta water; set aside.

2 Trim and core fennel. Chop fennel into 1-inch pieces. Snap off and discard woody bases from asparagus. Cut asparagus into 1-inch pieces. In a large skillet cook and stir fennel and asparagus in hot butter and olive oil over medium heat for 5 to 7 minutes or until nearly tender. Add garlic and cook 1 minute more.

3 Add cooked pasta, mascarpone cheese, and reserved pasta water to skillet. Gently stir to combine. Stir in mozzarella, Pecorino Romano, and peas. Season to taste with salt and pepper. Transfer to a serving dish and sprinkle with parsley.

Nutrition Facts per serving: 449 cal., 19 g total fat (9 g sat. fat), 41 mg chol., 430 mg sodium, 55 g carbo., 19 g pro.

linguine in fresh tomato
sauce WITH GARLIC-BASIL TOAST

Start to Finish: 20 minutes
Makes: 4 servings

10 ounces dried linguine

3 tablespoons olive oil

6 cloves garlic, minced or
   1 tablespoon bottled
   minced garlic

2 English muffins, split

¾ cup fresh basil, chopped

1 pint small tomatoes, halved

½ cup chicken broth or pasta
   water

1 teaspoon sugar

½ cup halved, pitted kalamata
   olives (optional)

   Grated Parmesan cheese;
   fresh basil (optional)

1 Heat broiler. Cook pasta according to package directions. Drain, set aside.

2 Meanwhile, in bowl combine 1 tablespoon of the oil and about one-third of the minced garlic; brush on cut sides of muffins. Place muffins on baking sheet. Broil, 3 to 4 inches from broiler, for 2 to 3 minutes, until golden. Sprinkle 1 tablespoon of the chopped basil; set aside.

3 In large saucepan heat remaining oil over medium-high. Add remaining garlic, basil, and tomatoes. Cook 2 minutes; add broth and sugar. Cook 3 to 4 minutes, until tomatoes soften. Season with salt and pepper. Stir in pasta and olives; heat through. Sprinkle cheese and basil.

4 Serve toasted muffins with pasta. Top with Parmesan and basil.

Nutrition Facts per serving: 450 cal., 12 g total fat (2 g sat. fat), 1 mg chol., 403 mg sodium, 72 g carbo., 12 g pro.

ravioli SKILLET

Start to Finish: 20 minutes
Makes: 4 (1⅔-cup) servings

1 **14.5-ounce can Italian-style stewed tomatoes, undrained**

½ **cup water**

2 **medium zucchini and/or yellow summer squash, halved lengthwise and cut into ½-inch-thick slices**

1 **9-ounce package refrigerated whole wheat four cheese ravioli**

1 **15- or 16-ounce can cannellini beans (white kidney beans) or navy beans, rinsed and drained**

2 **tablespoons snipped fresh basil or parsley**

2 **tablespoons finely shredded or grated Parmesan cheese**

1 In a very large skillet combine undrained tomatoes and the water; bring to boiling. Add zucchini and/or yellow summer squash and ravioli. Return to boiling; reduce heat. Cover and boil gently for 6 to 7 minutes or until ravioli is tender, stirring gently once or twice.

2 Stir beans into ravioli mixture; heat through. Sprinkle individual servings with basil and Parmesan cheese.

Nutrition Facts per serving: 305 cal., 8 g total fat (4 g sat. fat), 44 mg chol., 986 mg sodium, 49 g carbo., 18 g pro.

fusilli with garlic pesto
AND AGED PECORINO

Start to Finish: 35 minutes
Makes: 6 to 8 servings

15 cloves garlic, peeled

⅓ cup lightly packed fresh basil leaves

1 pound dried fusilli, gemelli, or tagliatelle pasta

½ cup olive oil

⅓ cup pine nuts, toasted

2 tablespoons finely shredded Pecorino Romano cheese (½ ounce)

¾ teaspoon sea salt

⅛ teaspoon freshly ground black pepper

1 cup small fresh basil leaves

¼ cup finely shredded Pecorino Romano cheese (1 ounce)

1 In a 5- to 6-quart Dutch oven cook garlic cloves in a large amount of boiling salted water for 8 minutes. Using a slotted spoon, transfer garlic to a blender. Add the ⅓ cup basil leaves to the boiling water and cook for 5 seconds; remove with slotted spoon and drain well on paper towels. (Do not drain boiling water.) Add basil to blender.

2 Add the pasta to the boiling water and cook according to package directions. Before draining pasta, remove ½ cup of the hot cooking water and set aside. Drain pasta; return to Dutch oven.

3 Meanwhile, for pesto: Add oil, 2 tablespoons of the pine nuts, the 2 tablespoons cheese, the salt, and pepper to blender. Cover and blend until nearly smooth (pesto will be thin).

4 Add pesto to cooked pasta; toss gently to coat. If necessary, toss in enough of the reserved cooking water to help coat the pasta evenly with pesto. Transfer pasta mixture to a serving bowl. Sprinkle with the 1 cup basil leaves, the ¼ cup cheese, and the remaining pine nuts. Serve immediately.*

Nutrition Facts per serving: 524 cal., 26 g total fat (4 g sat. fat), 5 mg chol., 264 mg sodium, 61 g carbo., 13 g pro.

***Tip:** The fresh basil leaves will darken if left on top of the hot pasta too long. To avoid this, serve the pasta right after adding the basil.

nutty orzo AND VEGETABLES

Start to Finish: 25 minutes
Makes: 4 servings

2 cups loose-pack frozen mixed
     vegetables

½ cup dried orzo pasta
     (rosamarina)

1 15-ounce can garbanzo beans
     (chickpeas), rinsed and
     drained

1 14.5-ounce can no-salt-added
     diced tomatoes, undrained

1⅓ cups purchased light
     spaghetti sauce

1 tablespoon snipped fresh
     thyme or 1 teaspoon dried
     thyme, crushed

¼ cup chopped cashews or
     slivered almonds, toasted

¼ cup shredded reduced-fat
     mozzarella cheese (1 ounce)

1 In a large saucepan cook the frozen vegetables and pasta according to pasta package directions, except omit any oil or salt. Drain. Return pasta mixture to hot saucepan.

2 Stir in garbanzo beans, undrained tomatoes, spaghetti sauce, and thyme. Bring to boiling; reduce heat. Cover and simmer for 5 minutes.

3 Stir in cashews. Sprinkle individual servings with mozzarella cheese.

Nutrition Facts per serving: 379 cal., 7 g total fat (2 g sat. fat), 3 mg chol., 453 mg sodium, 67 g carbo., 16 g pro.

pasta WITH SWISS CHARD

Start to Finish: 35 minutes
Makes: 2 servings

4 ounces dried whole grain
    bow tie or mostaccioli pasta

6 ounces fresh Swiss chard or
    spinach

1½ teaspoons olive oil

2 cloves garlic, minced

⅓ cup light ricotta cheese

2 tablespoons fat-free milk

2 tablespoons snipped fresh
    basil or 1 teaspoon dried
    basil, crushed

⅛ teaspoon salt

⅛ teaspoon black pepper
    Dash ground nutmeg

1 medium tomato, seeded and
    chopped

2 tablespoons shredded
    Parmesan cheese

1 Cook pasta according to package directions, except omit any oil or salt. Drain well. Return pasta to hot saucepan. Cover and keep warm.

2 Meanwhile, cut out and discard center ribs from Swiss chard or remove stems from spinach. Coarsely chop greens; set aside. In a large nonstick skillet heat oil over medium heat. Add garlic; cook for 15 seconds. Add Swiss chard or spinach. Cook over medium-low heat about 3 minutes or until greens are wilted and tender, stirring frequently. Stir in ricotta cheese, milk, basil, salt, pepper, and nutmeg. Cook and stir for 3 to 5 minutes more or until heated through.

3 Add the ricotta mixture and tomato to cooked pasta; toss gently to combine. Sprinkle individual servings with Parmesan cheese.

Nutrition Facts per serving: 307 cal., 8 g total fat (2 g sat. fat), 14 mg chol., 435 mg sodium, 51 g carbo., 14 g pro.

rigatoni WITH SHIITAKES, ARTICHOKES, AND PEPPERS

This pasta dinner combines a can of artichokes, sweet red peppers, and meaty shiitake mushrooms to create a beautifully rounded flavor.

Prep: 20 minutes
Cook: 25 minutes
Makes: 6 servings

3 **tablespoons olive oil**

⅓ **cup finely chopped shallots**

2 **red peppers, cut into thin strips**

½ **pound shiitake or white mushrooms, sliced**

1 **tablespoon finely chopped garlic**

1¼ **cups chicken broth**

1 **can (12 to 13.75 ounces) artichoke hearts, drained and quartered**

1 **teaspoon grated lemon peel**

3 **tablespoons fresh lemon juice**

1 **teaspoon salt**

¼ **teaspoon red pepper flakes**

¼ **teaspoon freshly ground pepper**

2 **tablespoons chopped fresh flat-leaf parsley**

1 **pound rigatoni, cooked according to package directions**

1 **cup freshly shredded Romano or Parmesan cheese**

1 Heat oil in 12-inch skillet over medium heat. Add shallots; cook 1 minute until lightly browned. Add peppers and mushrooms; cook 10 minutes, stirring occasionally, until vegetables are tender. Add garlic; cook 1 minute more.

2 Add broth, artichokes, lemon peel and juice, salt, red pepper, and ground pepper to skillet. Bring to boil; reduce heat and simmer 5 minutes. Stir in parsley

3 Toss hot pasta with sauce and Romano in large bowl.

Nutrition Facts per serving: 440 cal., 12 g total fat (3.5 g sat. fat), 14 mg chol., 770 mg sodium, 66 g carbo., 17 g pro.

gnocchi WITH MUSHROOM SAUCE

Prep: 30 minutes
Cook: 16 minutes
Stand: 15 minutes
Makes: 6 servings

2 ounces dried porcini mushrooms

Boiling water

⅓ cup thinly sliced leek (1 medium)

3 cloves garlic, minced

2 tablespoons butter

2 tablespoons olive oil

1½ pounds fresh portobello* and/or button mushrooms, sliced

1 pound fresh cremini mushrooms, sliced

¾ cup Chardonnay or other dry white wine

¾ teaspoon salt

¼ teaspoon ground black pepper

⅔ cup whipping cream

2 tablespoons all-purpose flour

1 tablespoon snipped fresh Italian (flat-leaf) parsley

2 16- or 17-ounce packages shelf-stable potato gnocchi

❶ Soak dried mushrooms in enough boiling water to cover about 15 minutes or until soft. Drain, discarding liquid. Squeeze mushrooms to remove additional liquid.

❷ Meanwhile, for mushroom sauce: In a 4- to 5-quart Dutch oven cook and stir leek and garlic in hot butter over medium heat for 2 minutes. Using a slotted spoon, remove leek mixture. Add oil to Dutch oven; heat over medium-high heat. Add porcini mushrooms, portobello and/or button mushrooms, and cremini mushrooms. Cook about 15 minutes or until mushrooms are lightly browned and liquid is evaporated, stirring occasionally. Stir in wine, salt, and pepper.

❸ In a small bowl whisk together cream and flour; stir into mushroom mixture. Cook and stir until thickened. Cook and stir for 1 minute more. Stir in leek mixture and parsley.

❹ Meanwhile, cook gnocchi according to package directions. Serve gnocchi with mushroom sauce.

Nutrition Facts per serving: 543 cal., 20 g total fat (10 g sat. fat), 47 mg chol., 878 mg sodium, 78 g carbo., 13 g pro.

*Tip: For a lighter colored sauce, use a knife or a teaspoon to gently scrape away the gills (the black portions underneath the caps) from the portobello mushrooms before slicing.

fettuccine-vegetable TOSS

Colorful and flavor-packed, be sure to spear a bit of each ingredient with every forkful to enjoy this one-dish meal to the fullest.

Start to Finish: 20 minutes
Makes: 4 servings

1   **9-ounce package refrigerated spinach fettuccine**

1   **tablespoon olive oil**

2   **tablespoons chopped green onion (1)**

2   **cups chopped red and/or yellow tomatoes (4 medium)**

½   **cup finely chopped carrot (1 medium)**

¼   **cup oil-packed dried tomatoes, drained and snipped**

½   **cup crumbled garlic-and-herb feta cheese, peppercorn feta cheese, or plain feta cheese (2 ounces)**

❶ Cook pasta according to package directions; drain well. Return to hot pan; cover and keep warm.

❷ Meanwhile, in a large skillet heat oil over medium heat. Add green onion; cook for 30 seconds. Stir in fresh tomatoes, carrot, and dried tomatoes. Cover and cook for 5 minutes, stirring once. Spoon tomato mixture over cooked pasta. Sprinkle with feta cheese; toss gently.

Nutrition Facts per serving: 311 cal., 11 g total fat (4 g sat. fat), 73 mg chol., 250 mg sodium, 44 g carbo., 13 g pro.

linguine WITH GORGONZOLA SAUCE

Start to Finish: 25 minutes
Makes: 4 servings

1 **9-ounce package refrigerated whole wheat linguine**

1 **pound fresh asparagus, trimmed and cut into 2-inch-long pieces**

1 **cup evaporated fat-free milk**

2 **ounces reduced-fat cream cheese (Neufchâtel), cubed**

2 **ounces Gorgonzola or other blue cheese, crumbled (½ cup)**

¼ **teaspoon salt**

2 **tablespoons chopped walnuts, toasted**

1 Cook pasta and asparagus according to package directions; drain well. Return pasta and asparagus to pan. Cover and keep warm.

2 Meanwhile, for sauce, in a medium saucepan combine milk, cream cheese, half of the Gorgonzola cheese, and the salt. Bring to boiling over medium heat, whisking constantly; reduce heat. Simmer, uncovered, for 2 minutes, stirring frequently (sauce may appear slightly curdled).

3 Pour sauce over pasta mixture; toss gently to coat. Transfer to four shallow bowls. Sprinkle individual servings with remaining Gorgonzola cheese and the walnuts. Serve immediately (sauce will thicken upon standing).

Nutrition Facts per serving: 361 cal., 13 g total fat (6 g sat. fat), 42 mg chol., 476 mg sodium, 44 g carbo., 19 g pro.

teriyaki PENNE

Tossed with pasta tubes, this easy Asian stir-fry delivers a tasty bonus with every bite. The zippy ginger-spiked sauce coats the pasta inside and out for a double dose of flavor.

Start to Finish: 25 minutes
Makes: 4 servings

8 **ounces dried tomato-basil penne or plain penne pasta**

½ **teaspoon grated fresh ginger**

1 **clove garlic, minced**

1 **tablespoon toasted sesame oil or cooking oil**

3 **cups packaged shredded broccoli (broccoli slaw mix)**

2 **cups sliced fresh mushrooms**

¼ **cup teriyaki sauce**

¼ **cup thinly sliced green onions**

1 Cook pasta according to package directions; drain. Return pasta to saucepan.

2 Meanwhile, in a large skillet cook ginger and garlic in hot oil for 15 seconds. Stir in shredded broccoli, mushrooms, and teriyaki sauce. Cook and stir about 5 minutes or until broccoli is crisp-tender.

3 To serve, add broccoli mixture to hot pasta; toss gently to combine. Sprinkle with green onions.

Nutrition Facts per serving: 286 cal., 5 g total fat (1 g sat. fat), 0 mg chol., 749 mg sodium, 50 g carbo., 11 g pro.

tofu stir-fry WITH SOBA NOODLES

Be sure to use firm tub-style tofu for this sensational stir-fry. The pieces will hold their shape better during cooking than softer styles of tofu.

Start to Finish: 25 minutes
Makes: 4 servings

- 5 ounces soba noodles (buckwheat noodles)
- 2 teaspoons toasted sesame oil
- 2 cloves garlic, minced
- 1 teaspoon grated fresh ginger
- 1 large red sweet pepper, coarsely chopped
- 12 ounces firm tub-style tofu (fresh bean curd), drained and cubed
- 4 cups fresh baby spinach leaves
- 3 tablespoons reduced-sodium teriyaki sauce
- 1 tablespoon water
- 3 tablespoons snipped fresh cilantro or basil

1 Cook soba noodles according to package directions; drain and set aside. Meanwhile, in a large skillet heat sesame oil over medium-high heat. Add garlic and ginger; cook and stir for 30 seconds. Add sweet pepper. Cook and stir for 2 minutes. Add tofu; cook and stir for 1 minute more.

2 Add spinach, teriyaki sauce, and the water; stir until spinach is wilted. Add cooked soba noodles and cilantro; heat through, stirring gently to coat.

Nutrition Facts per serving: 294 cal., 10 g total fat (1 g sat. fat), 0 mg chol., 648 mg sodium, 36 g carbo., 21 g pro.

metric information

The charts on this page provide a guide for converting measurements from the U.S. customary system, which is used throughout this book, to the metric system.

PRODUCT DIFFERENCES

Most of the ingredients called for in the recipes in this book are available in most countries. However, some are known by different names. Here are some common American ingredients and their possible counterparts:

- Sugar (white) is granulated, fine granulated, or castor sugar.
- Powdered sugar is icing sugar.
- All-purpose flour is enriched, bleached, or unbleached white household flour. When self-rising flour is used in place of all-purpose flour in a recipe that calls for leavening, omit the leavening agent (baking soda or baking powder) and salt.
- Light-color corn syrup is golden syrup.
- Cornstarch is cornflour.
- Baking soda is bicarbonate of soda.
- Vanilla or vanilla extract is vanilla essence.
- Green, red, or yellow sweet peppers are capsicums or bell peppers.
- Golden raisins are sultanas.

VOLUME AND WEIGHT

The United States traditionally uses cup measures for liquid and solid ingredients. The chart, top right, shows the approximate imperial and metric equivalents. If you are accustomed to weighing solid ingredients, the following approximate equivalents will be helpful.

- 1 cup butter, castor sugar, or rice = 8 ounces = $\frac{1}{2}$ pound = 250 grams
- 1 cup flour = 4 ounces = $\frac{1}{4}$ pound = 125 grams
- 1 cup icing sugar = 5 ounces = 150 grams

Canadian and U.S. volume for a cup measure is 8 fluid ounces (237 ml), but the standard metric equivalent is 250 ml.

1 British imperial cup is 10 fluid ounces.

In Australia, 1 tablespoon equals 20 ml, and there are 4 teaspoons in the Australian tablespoon.

Spoon measures are used for smaller amounts of ingredients. Although the size of the tablespoon varies slightly in different countries, for practical purposes and for recipes in this book, a straight substitution is all that's necessary. Measurements made using cups or spoons always should be level unless stated otherwise.

COMMON WEIGHT RANGE REPLACEMENTS

Imperial / U.S.	Metric
$\frac{1}{2}$ ounce	15 g
1 ounce	25 g or 30 g
4 ounces ($\frac{1}{4}$ pound)	115 g or 125 g
8 ounces ($\frac{1}{2}$ pound)	225 g or 250 g
16 ounces (1 pound)	450 g or 500 g
$1\frac{1}{4}$ pounds	625 g
$1\frac{1}{2}$ pounds	750 g
2 pounds or $2\frac{1}{4}$ pounds	1,000 g or 1 Kg

OVEN TEMPERATURE EQUIVALENTS

Fahrenheit Setting	Celsius Setting*	Gas Setting
300°F	150°C	Gas Mark 2 (very low)
325°F	160°C	Gas Mark 3 (low)
350°F	180°C	Gas Mark 4 (moderate)
375°F	190°C	Gas Mark 5 (moderate)
400°F	200°C	Gas Mark 6 (hot)
425°F	220°C	Gas Mark 7 (hot)
450°F	230°C	Gas Mark 8 (very hot)
475°F	240°C	Gas Mark 9 (very hot)
500°F	260°C	Gas Mark 10 (extremely hot)
Broil	Broil	Grill

*Electric and gas ovens may be calibrated using celsius. However, for an electric oven, increase celsius setting 10 to 20 degrees when cooking above 160°C. For convection or forced air ovens (gas or electric) lower the temperature setting 25°F/10°C when cooking at all heat levels.

BAKING PAN SIZES

Imperial / U.S.	Metric
9×1$\frac{1}{2}$-inch round cake pan	22- or 23×4-cm (1.5 L)
9×1$\frac{1}{2}$-inch pie plate	22- or 23×4-cm (1 L)
8×8×2-inch square cake pan	20×5-cm (2 L)
9×9×2-inch square cake pan	22- or 23×4.5-cm (2.5 L)
11×7×1$\frac{1}{2}$-inch baking pan	28×17×4-cm (2 L)
2-quart rectangular baking pan	30×19×4.5-cm (3 L)
13×9×2-inch baking pan	34×22×4.5-cm (3.5 L)
15×10×1-inch jelly roll pan	40×25×2-cm
9×5×3-inch loaf pan	23×13×8-cm (2 L)
2-quart casserole	2 L

U.S. / STANDARD METRIC EQUIVALENTS

$\frac{1}{8}$ teaspoon = 0.5 ml	$\frac{1}{3}$ cup = 3 fluid ounces = 75 ml
$\frac{1}{4}$ teaspoon = 1 ml	$\frac{1}{2}$ cup = 4 fluid ounces = 125 ml
$\frac{1}{2}$ teaspoon = 2 ml	$\frac{1}{3}$ cup = 5 fluid ounces = 150 ml
1 teaspoon = 5 ml	$\frac{3}{4}$ cup = 6 fluid ounces = 175 ml
1 tablespoon = 15 ml	1 cup = 8 fluid ounces = 250 ml
2 tablespoons = 25 ml	2 cups = 1 pint = 500 ml
$\frac{1}{4}$ cup = 2 fluid ounces = 50 ml	1 quart = 1 litre

index

Note: Page references in *italics* refer to photographs.

239